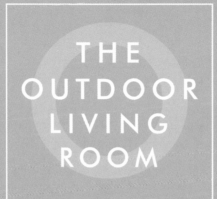

THE OUTDOOR LIVING ROOM

THE OUTDOOR LIVING ROOM

MARTHA BAKER

PHOTOGRAPHS BY CHUCK BAKER

TEXT BY SARA EVANS

CLARKSON POTTER/PUBLISHERS

NEW YORK

Published by Clarkson Potter/Publishers, New York, New York.
Member of the Crown Publishing Group.

Random House, Inc. New York, Toronto, London, Sydney, Auckland
www.randomhouse.com

CLARKSON N. POTTER is a trademark and Potter and colophon are
registered trademarks of Random House, Inc.

Printed in China

Design by Wayne Wolf/Blue Cup Design, Inc.

Library of Congress Cataloging-in-Publication Data
Baker, Martha.
The outdoor living room / by Martha Baker ;
photographs by Chuck Baker.— 1st ed.
1. Outdoor living spaces—Decoration—
United States.   I. Baker, Chuck.   II. Title.
NK2117 B35 2001
747—dc21   00–055735

ISBN 0-609-60646-8

10 9 8 7 6 5 4 3 2 1

First Edition

ACKNOWLEDGMENTS

The Outdoor Living Room is a book about magical places and personal spaces that some people actually live in and the rest of us only dream about. Every garden and porch and patio in this book is here because a wonderful individual or family decided to share their home with me. How fortunate I am to have met so many lovely people, who not only invited us in, but later were enthused about the project that they took the time out to introduce me to their friends down the road with equally fantastic homes. This book has been an exciting experience for me because of all the new friends that made it possible, and I can't thank them enough.

How can I forget Jennifer Garraguies, who introduced us to Palm Beach, or Susan and Dennis Richards, who wined and dined us in Miami? What an amazing experience it was to sit on the porch with nonagenerian Mary Ford and then have her drive us to dinner in her vintage Bentley. Ken Farrah and Dee Ann Carol helped us to discover Windsor. Susan Glass spent days sharing Northern Michigan with us, and Greenwich, Connecticut feels like home because of Charlotte Sickles, Memory Lewis, and Alease Fisher.

Thanks especially to my helpful friend and agent, Deborah Geltman who is always available to answer my questions, and to my editor Margot Schupf at Clarkson Potter for her Herculean efforts. I also want to acknowledge the input of Wayne Wolf, Marysarah Quinn, Lauren Shakely, Sara Evans, and Annetta Hanna. My husband, Chuck, once again brought these outdoor spaces to life with his masterful photography and a big thanks to my four children, Jesse, Emily, Charlie, and Hannah for putting up with me through the process.

CONTENTS

INTRODUCTION

Our summer life together started back in the 1970s, the first summer we rented "Belle Buoy,"—a tiny cottage and a barn on an overgrown stretch of land on the North Fork of Long Island, fifteen acres of untamed heaven. "Belle Buoy" was secluded, wild and tangled, but came with its own beach and with dazzling views stretching across Great Peconic Bay to Shelter Island and to the South Fork beyond..

I had returned from a winter of working abroad and discovered that, in a wildly extravagant and romantic gesture, Chuck had rented the whole property, house and barn, land and beach, as a surprise for me.

It was during those first summers together that we discovered the joys of living outdoors. Chuck, my son Jesse, and I were outside from the time we awoke until bedtime, walking the property and playing on the beach. Life was relaxed and different, both

in quantity and quality, with no structured playdates or heavy-duty housekeeping. We awoke to birds, not trucks. Our days both flew by and lasted forever.

The house itself, with its almost nonexistent kitchen, was too tiny for entertaining. I naturally longed for an outdoor space where we could welcome our friends. Off the living room, flanked by two overgrown flower beds, were a few steps. A few more steps led down to a second level, the remnant of an enclosed formal garden.

Although it had fallen into disrepair, this garden had great bones, with low brick ivy-covered walls lined by flower beds and four other beds divided by antique bricks. The focal point was an old, oval cement fish pond, about five feet by three and a half. It had no running water and hadn't seen a fish in fifty years. Each evening, we would heat up four giant pots of water in the kitchen and rush them outdoors to fill up the pond. Sitting in our makeshift hot tub, drinks in hand, eye level with the wild garden, we would talk and dream with our friends under the stars.

The enclosed garden at Belle Buoy, with its magical fish pond, was an experiment in living outdoors. During our happy summers there, Chuck and I came to realize that wonderful spaces can be created from almost nothing but imagination. It was an epiphany: *This is a great way to live.*

After five summers of renting on the North Fork, it became clear to us that it was time to buy our own place and put down our summer roots. Often we would take the little ferry from Belle Buoy over to Shelter Island

and walk through the Victorian village of Shelter Island Heights. We marveled at how lovely it was. The carpenter Gothic houses, remnants of a nineteenth-century Methodist retreat, are set cheek-by-jowl on streets that tumble down to the harbor or are clustered around the sweeping village green. To me it represents a way of life that used to be, a place where our kids could roam and wander, swim and sail, through all the bright days of summer. The village had the feel of an old, European town, with spaces that tapered from private to semiprivate to public, a real community, a place where much of the land is owned and used by everyone.

These were my requirements: a house in the Heights that was totally unrenovated and had a wraparound porch and a tower. The first house the realtor showed us, on a cold November day, fit the bill. And for many summers, with our growing family, we sailed in the harbor and around the island, and played on tennis courts that were right down the hill. We joined the little beach club on the bay with its candy-striped awnings, where we whiled away the afternoons while the kids swam and played in the sand. We set up a Sunday baseball game on the village green. It was a life that approached perfection, a life out of time.

When we first bought it, the house was a wreck. It had been abandoned for years and inside there were yards of lime-green shag carpeting. We soon discovered that there was no interior access to the tower. And the porch of our dreams was a mess. It had been disastrously modernized sometime in the 1950s and was totally rotten. All around us, everyone was living out on their porches,

from May until Labor Day. So we set about rebuilding ours from scratch.

Chuck and I wanted to build a porch that would be right for our 1875 house, one that would honor the spirit of its original architecture. Following the footprint of the original porch, we created a design of repeating Gothic arches that echoed the shapes of the windows and doors. We put up wainscoting on the ceiling, painted it a gentle, celadon green, and hung old-fashioned ceiling fans. We laid and oiled new wooden floors. Function was an important factor in how we organized this space: the living area was just off the living room; the eating area was a few steps from the kitchen. Next, we created a new front entrance, using old brick for terracing the steep front yard down to the street level. In creating architecture without an architect, Chuck and I came to realize that we enjoy making our own discoveries—and our own mistakes.

We decided to throw the symmetry of the original porch off a little by creating a hexagonal gazebo on the front corner. This area immediately became our new outdoor living room. It was the most flexible space imaginable, sometimes serving as a dining room, sometimes as a place to play board games or just to sit quietly and read. Often, it was the perfect place to sit with guests. Temporarily stripped of its furniture, it became a place where the kids could really get going without slamming into anything. We built window boxes that straddled the tops of the railings and hung an old swing from the ceiling. The porch was very shady, so we grew only impatiens, but those simple flowers provided us with wonderful privacy. At night, we would string fish lights all across the porch to create a magical summer space.

Off one side of the porch, we created a transitional space by building a patio that connected our new kitchen wing to the dining side of the porch. We laid leftover bricks around an old, slate slab that we found buried on the property and put out a table and chairs. Overlooking the small garden, this patio was ideal for dining and entertaining, a place to sit when we craved the warmth of the sun and a better view of the birds and flowers.

Many people tend to set their furniture in one place, and then leave it, especially in a summer home. Perhaps that's because they only spend a few months there. But because I'm a stylist and an editor, I have a powerful impulse to mix things up and change them, to constantly create new rooms and new settings. For me, our living space is a stage on which the sets are always changing, where we play out the comedies and dramas of our family and our lives.

Families outgrow houses; we eventually outgrew this cherished home. With four kids and lots of guests, Chuck and I felt that we were bursting at the seams. In another area of Shelter Island we found an abandoned stucco house right on the water, dating from the 1920s. We would bike over there and daydream about what it would be like to own it. It had its own dock and a private beach; we knew it was perfect for our family as our kids all love to sail. The idea of being right on the water, watching the boats coming in and out of the harbor, and drinking in the

sunset each summer evening over the waters of Great Peconic was irresistible.

The new old house was also an unspeakable wreck. Neglected for ten years, it needed everything—a new roof, new windows, walls, wiring, and plumbing. We left the veranda until last—our dream veranda, that still, due to unresolved zoning issues, has not been built. But, as is often the case, our situation has had an upside. Not having a porch has forced us to become ever more resourceful about our outdoor living space. We are constantly discovering new ways to use other areas, ways I imagine we would never consider if we actually had built what we wanted. Instead, we have created a whole series of evolving outdoor living spaces that don't lock us in to one way of doing or being. We painted the outer walls of the house a soft peachy-yellow, a shade that evokes old stucco houses in the south of France. These layers of color provide a perfect backdrop for the exterior living space.

We designed a kitchen addition onto the 1920s house which helped to create a room-scale courtyard, a perfect spot for day-in, day-out outdoor living. We've added old stone benches and comfortable seating, painted our antique French garden chairs a classic dark green, and placed big terra-cotta containers of flowers around. A garden on wheels that is constantly on the move, depending on whim and need, these containers provide an ideal way to redefine and reshape our entertaining space. Completely sheltered from the fierce winds that often blow

ABOVE L TO R: The redesigned porch with its sprung arches echoing the carpenter gothic, 1875 architecture of our first house, was where we lived all summer. The addition of the gazebo at one end threw off the symmetry of the space in a pleasing way, while providing yet another room, a flexible area for dining or reading or idly swinging on the old, bentwood swing. Our springform French garden furniture was painted white to match the porch and the elaborate trim of the house.

from the bay, this courtyard has become a haven. We built one continuous window box that stretches across the back of the house, spanning twenty windows, including the garage. This window box functions as an important architectural element, visually pulling the house together into one unified space, while providing flowers and greenery for the eye, and fragrant herbs for our kitchen.

Realizing that it might take forever to get this house just right, I comforted myself by planting a seaside garden the very first spring we were there. Our daughter, Hannah, dug her very own garden because she insisted on a garden that is an exuberant mix of vegetables and annuals.

Chuck and I also made a wide path of old brick leading right down to the water, a path roomy enough to provide still more seating. There's an old iron bench on the path, under rebar arches that in summer are a bower of Eden roses, clematis *montana rubens,* and ivy that all grow so thickly that the bench is almost covered, creating an amusing topiary.

The impulse to redesign our outdoor stage sets has never left us. We pitch tents near the water and set up a dining table. We carry pots of plants down and grill dinner right on our beach. Sometimes the theme is simply summer; sometimes we fling camouflage nets over an inexpensive tent. We often use plants as a quick way to redecorate. For instance, for our tropical phase, we set vibrant green banana plants and bright canna lilies in fiberglass planters that look like old, rusted iron and

ABOVE: We created a delightful temporary outdoor dining room, right at the water's edge, using moss-covered tree stumps for seating and inexpensive army-navy store camouflage fabric and mosquito netting.

RIGHT: We paved our patio with stained concrete inlaid with patterns of stars and borders created with local beach stones.

FACING PAGE: In our courtyard just off the kitchen, we had clay pots filled with herbs, a portable kitchen garden, punctuated with bright, windowbox annuals.

ABOVE: Our daughter Hannah, looking fresh from the south seas, arranged the flowers.

arranged them all around the table to create an island paradise.

Each time we have created a new space, it's been a lesson in richness, a lesson in the joys of living outdoors. No matter where we have lived, we have carved out spaces where we've spent every waking minute. With each successive move, and over the course of many summers, we have discovered the infinite pleasures—and the fun—of creating outdoor rooms to live in. Sometimes they've worked for a whole summer, sometimes for a week or two, sometimes just for a night.

Chuck and I have come to realize that no matter where one lives from Monday through Friday, the time that really counts in the summer is the time spent out of doors. It's about all that daylight, all that air, the smells of summer, the flowers. It's

about time with your children that's relaxed and free and not restricted by walls. Another of the best things about al fresco living rooms is that they don't need cleaning.

Chuck and I have traveled around the country, visiting and photographing people in their summer living rooms. We've joined them on their porches and patios, terraces and verandas, and in and around their pools, experiencing the many ways they live their fair-weather lives. The result, this book, is filled with ideas and resources that will inspire you to think creatively about your own summer environments. We hope you will discover, as we have, countless ways to extend both the fun—and the infinite joys—of living outdoors.

M

MODERN

In modern environments, less is definitely more. Basic design elements get enormous play and raw, industrial or hard-edged materials such as metals or rendered stone are very important. Many modern outdoor spaces engender a spirit of contemplation as their very lack of clutter inspires meditation. And here's another revelation—minimalist environments require minimal maintenance.

SERENISSIMA

This contemporary Miami home is the quintessence of Florida design. The house, which faces Key Biscayne, and its surroundings were designed by architects Teofilo Victoria and Maria de la Guardia as a tribute to Venice. Like the palazzos on the Venetian canals, this house fronts the Bay. An island sits in the middle of the rectangular Grand Canal pool, with a bright red bridge that symbolizes the intricate system of bridges and canals of Venice itself. On the island stand four towering streetlamps, just like the ones used to tie up Venetian gondolas.

Color is what Ca Ziff is all about. Built ten years ago, when the rest of Miami was awash in peach and pink, the architects instead opted for an intense palette of red and ochre, shades that are common to Tuscany and that come from the iron oxides in the earth itself. These hues are emphasized by the tropical turquoise of the pools and the cobalt shade of the sky.

Planted in a grid, a stately grove of Royal palms forms a natural canopy overlooking the bay. Densely carpeted with zoysia grass, the outdoor dining room consists of a large cooking area that is often used for entertainining, with big old teak tables set out under the filtered light of the palms. *Ficus repens*, a miniature ficus vine, covers and softens walls and staircases with elegant greenery.

LEFT: The arched red bridge over the canal that links house to pool reinforces the Venetian design theme of this unusual home, its intense hues a stunning contrast to its pastel Miami neighbors.

ABOVE: All the outdoor accessories, such as handthrown Tuscan planters and European wrought-iron furniture have been chosen to add an authentic Italian touch.

FACING PAGE: An outdoor shower set into a terra cotta wall. A vine-covered wall and staircase frame and soften the pool.

ABOVE: The sparkling, turquoise water of the pool at Ca Ziff conjures up memories of summer days at the Lido and the magical dazzle of Venice.

RIGHT: A wrought-iron chair from the renowned Hervé Baume collection was made in France. The bottom of the pool is visible through this arched doorway.

THE SHELTERING SKY

This stucco house in Miami cried out for an exterior that would reflect its Mediterranean style, which is well suited to the area's tropical climate.

ABOVE: Arching arbors and intricate, wrought iron decorative elements all bring necessary shade and coolness to the outdoor living areas.

FACING PAGE: The stark white walls and staircase against the cobalt of the winter sky create a perfect interaction between structure and nature.

Landscape designer Harry Nelson was called upon to plan an environment that would complement the architecture of the house. He moved the spirit of the house outdoors with his lavish use of blue and green mosaic tiles—on pots holding palms, on the top of the dining table, on the risers of the terrace steps, and in the pool. Artisan Luciano Frenchi created the mosaics and also painted Islamic graphics onto the pots.

This home is occupied each year from November to April, making the sheltered porch an absolute necessity, a place to get away from the intensity of the Miami sun. Coming here is a lot like spending an afternoon in north Africa—everything, from the intricate metal cutouts on the circular fence and the gate enclosing the pool, from the white pillars and splashing fountains, to the blue-domed gazebo, evokes an exotic feel. Another terrace sits at the top of a long, stark, white stucco staircase, leading to another outdoor space just off the master bedroom.

On most Sundays there is a barbecue with friends and their dogs all splashing around in the pool. At night, Moroccan lanterns placed all around the terraces cast an intricate pattern of shadows. Deep-blue cushions and awnings, piped in white, further emphasize the exotic feel of this magical home.

ABOVE L TO R: At night, candles set inside these intricately crafted lanterns give off a wonderful light. This modern waterfall comes from a water track at one end of the pool, and makes a continual soothing sound. An orchid grows out of a piece of petrifed wood.

FACING PAGE: Surrounded by rustling palm trees, a domed, mosque-like gazebo with built-in benches is perfect in keeping with the North African ambience of this home.

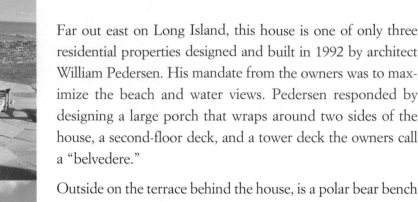

BLUESTONE SPECIAL

ABOVE: Architect Willliam Pederson used bluestone for walls, terraces, and paving for this intriguing contemporary home. The broad fields, sea, and sky of Long Island's East End give this property a feeling of infinite space.

FACING PAGE The curving wall and gravel path serve a dual visual function, leading eyes and feet both toward the house with its surprising terraces, decks, and turrets, and toward the horizon.

Far out east on Long Island, this house is one of only three residential properties designed and built in 1992 by architect William Pedersen. His mandate from the owners was to maximize the beach and water views. Pedersen responded by designing a large porch that wraps around two sides of the house, a second-floor deck, and a tower deck the owners call a "belvedere."

Outside on the terrace behind the house, is a polar bear bench sculpted by Judy McKie, a piece that marries art and utility. The first floor porch has 1950s white-painted metal lawn furniture, a style also found in dark green on the ground-floor front porch. A round, ceramic-tiled table from the town of Deruta in Italy sits on the front porch, along with a hammock found in a local hardware store.

In this home life is lived outside, weather permitting. Breakfasts are eaten on the terraces, lunches enjoyed on the ground-floor long porch overlooking a small, freshwater pond, and hurricane-lamp lit dinners served in the belvedere. The lap pool, housed in what was formerly an attached garage, is a simple, prefabricated "swim against the current" version. In summer, the doors are thrown open, so that swimmers feel they are actually outdoors, but because it's enclosed this pool can also be used all winter long.

Bluestone has always had magical qualities, ever since it was used as a key material in the construction of Stonehenge. The house uses bluestone in myriad ways: it forms the base of the house and the chimney and is also used as terrace paving. A long, curving wall made to resemble drystack is actually built from cut bluestone over masonry. This wall, which links the house to the landscape, has the comforting look of having been there a long time.

ABOVE: The large downstairs porch that wraps around two sides of this contemporary beach house combines both welcome shade and vast, open vistas.

RIGHT: William Pedersen created an open deck which the owners call the "belvedere." This tower is in perfect perpendicular contrast to the flatness of the Long Island horizon.

ABOVE: The lap pool provides all-season, indoor/outdoor exercise. When the doors are open during warm weather, swimmers experience a sense of swimming in the tidewater bay that flows just beyond the lawn.

RIGHT: Set on an open deck overlooking the water, a classic teakwood steamer chair recalls an ocean voyage far out at sea.

LEFT: Light and shadow play off each other, shifting and changing with each season.

BELOW: Judy McKie's polar bear sculpture, cut and shaped from stone, does double-duty as a bench on the back terrace.

RIGHT: 1950s metal lawn chairs painted a dark shade of green evoke the owner's suburban childhood. This house is a virtual museum, both indoors and out, of iconic studio furniture, most of which was discovered at Pritam & Eames in nearby East Hampton.

ABOVE LEFT: The afternoon sun shines through these refinished, white metal French lawn chairs, dating from the 1950s. The chairs function both as comfortable rockers and as imposing sculpture. All around the house the grounds seem natural and untouched; the house is set in a landscape that speaks for itself.

ABOVE: Set on the second-floor porch (a favorite place to have breakfast), traditional English-style teak garden chairs contrast with the cubist form of the blue-stone chimney and the rounded, cedar-clad, contemporary architectural forms of the tower. The stark, bright light plays against the dense, almost palpable shadows.

SHEER MAGIC

Influenced by the work of Richard Meier, architect Gustavo Ramos created a Florida haven for German gallery owner Gert Elfering and his wife, who, with their young son, spend their winters in the Florida sun.

When the couple bought the house in 1996, a rectangular porch at the back faced the canal. This area was enlarged into a generous curve and imaginatively hung with sheer curtains mounted on a track that follows the curve of the porch. At night, when pulled, these curtains not only keep out mosquitoes but also give an enchanted feel to the space.

The sheer curtains, along with such elements as a ceiling fan (its wooden blades painted to look like silver), Philippe Stark chairs draped in white duck, and silver-painted columns, all combine to create a postmodern sense of comfort and tradition in the outdoor living areas of this home.

In keeping with its minimalist intent, only six chairs and a round table set with an elegant vase filled with white roses sit on the porch. This careful editing lends a beautiful tranquillity, a distilled sense of consummate simplicity. The pool echoes this theme, with its childproof fence of metal and netting, a fence that can be removed for grown-up parties.

The upper decks of the house are bordered with industrial steel railings, a material that echoes the walled entrance with its stainless steel gate. The gate plays off the coral walkways beautifully, as does the fountain at the entrance, a subtle play of natural elements, water, stone, and light.

ABOVE. Architect Gustavo Ramos created borders of stainless steel for the outside railings of the Elfering winter home in Florida, one of many architectural elements inspired by the work of Richard Meier.

FACING PAGE: The Elfering's young son plays peek-a-boo from behind the sheer curtains that are hung from a track surrounding the perimeter of the rounded portico.

CLOCKWISE FROM LEFT:
The outside gates fabricated
from stainless steel, the simple
white track-hung curtains, chairs
covered with removable—and
washable—cotton duck, and a
wood-and-metal ceiling fan all
work together for ease of use
while reinforcing the architectural integrity of this home.

FACING PAGE: Ramos
added industrial railings fabricated from stainless steel to the
upper decks overlooking the
swimming pool. Like the other
metal details, these railings
accentuate the simplicity and
consummate modernity of the
house.

FACING PAGE: The furnishings of the porch are both minimalist and elegant, just a set of
simple chairs by Phillipe Stark
arranged around a glass-
topped metal table.

MODERN IDEAS

TOP RIGHT: These planters were fabricated from stainless steel, a hi-tech material used in a tradtional manner.

ABOVE: The perfect arc of this metal handrail was inspired by the Delano Hotel in Miami. The simple, graphic shape reflects perfectly in the water below.

RIGHT: This circular hot tub contrasts with the horizonality of the wall and ocean, and tall palms around it.

ABOVE CENTER: A curving water channel runs along the outside of this home, fed by circulating water falling from a series of stainless steel cylinders set into the exterior walls.

RIGHT: An inflatable chair and hassock, in bright primary blue, is sturdier than its beanbag inspiration and has the added advvantage of being collapsible.

RIGHT: A riff on a tradtional deck chair, this practical version is made from weatherproof, white-coated aluminum, with a modernist black cover. It is lightweight and folds up for easy storage.

ABOVE: This pool ladder was fabricated from plumbing pipe. It is both strong and practical—and a change from the aluminum norm.

LEFT: A space-saving resistance lap pool, set in simple, wooden decking, is a high-tech invention that here functions as an indoor/outdoor exercise venue, depending on the season.

LEFT: A simple, track fountain set at one end of a pool becomes a major water feature as its scultural arcs play and move in the sun.

PAVING

The decision of how to pave our outdoor rooms is as important as choosing interior flooring. In practical terms, outdoor flooring makes spaces habitable and prevents us from sinking knee-deep in mud. Design-wise it can reinforce the style of each area and visually pull spaces together. Today the choice of materials available is extraordinary and most are appropriate to any setting. We may choose whimsical stone footprints or bright ceramic tiles. Tranquil Zen stepping stones set in gravel or blue-stones geometrically placed on grass are just the ticket for in-town or modern areas. Antique bricks or painted wooden veranda floors are ideal for romantic or traditional homes, evoking another time. Teak, cedar, or wood chips can create a rustic pathway. A more recent innovation, stamped and tinted concrete, can be fabricated to resemble slate, Belgian block, and a range of cut stones, which makes it a practical and affordable solution to almost any paving dilemma.

TOP: 1. Different paving spaces to define different sitting/eating areas of outdoor space **FACING PAGE: 2.** Tiles and corals combined **3.** Patio with cement edged in tile **4.** Cement scored and stained to look like limestone **5.** Cement molded footpath **6.** Irregular stones set in mondo grass **7.** Bluestone cut in unusual way **8.** Coral pavers edged in grass **9.** Tile porch floor c. 1940s

1-2. Two ways of using wood bleach or age naturally 3. Brick laid in herringbone pattern 4. Belgian block as an edging detail 5. Whimsical edging 6. Pavers with wide areas of grass between them—contrast in texture 7. Different sizes, colors of pavers 8. Gravel path with crisp edging—played against the texture of groundcover 9-10. Natural stone paths cut in squares or natural shapes 11. Oil and stone type of gravel courtyard 12. Decorative pebble paving 13. Old moldy lime-

stone pavers from France **14.** Cedar tree logs cut into 2" disks, laid in the sand **15.** Grey "brick" pavers set on narrow edge **16.** Hardwood mulch path **17-18.** Decorative pattern with grass veins **19.** Millstones used as path **20.** Recycled rubber made into roof terrace pavers **21.** Bluestone pavers with herbs planted between **22.** Bluestone patio⁻

C

CLASSIC

"To summer" is a uniquely American verb,
one that encompasses not just a time of year
but a way of life. It is this season, the classic
American summer, that we celebrate here.
Combining the age-old stylistic elements of
classicism—those of symmetry, proportion,
and balance—with such traditional outdoor
materials as stone, brick, and terra cotta, these
homes come close to achieving the ultimate
classical ideal: complete harmony with nature.

FROM THE TERRACE...

The urge to gather around a fire is a deeply primal one. This 1920s brick Georgian-style home in Connecticut boasts not just one but two impressive outdoor fireplaces. When the design firm of David Easton/Eric Smith undertook the extensive renovation of the property a few years ago, they created both a sophisticated alcove cooking center and an accompanying fireplace with seating and storage bins on either side. Easton and Smith combined softly hued brick with terra-cotta tiles from France in the fireplace surrounds, evoking a European feel. To age these materials, Smith used a common architecture's potion of yogurt, sour milk, and manure. The cutouts in both chimneys function as intriguing design elements, breaking up mass and allowing light to pass through. Spotlights placed in the ravine behind the fireplace provide dramatic illumination when darkness falls. In every season, the fireplaces draw people to their warmth and light. Stretching the boundaries of the physical house, this outdoor entertaining space represents a growing and significant design trend.

Easton and Smith created a large, bluestone terrace spanning the entire length of the rear of the house. Spacious enough to incorporate both a living and a dining area, this terrace is a perfect example of how outdoor space can seamlessly extend interior function. The cooking and dining areas are adjacent to the indoor kitchen, while the terrace living area serves as a virtual addition to the living room of the home.

Careful planning and design have created a continuous series of descending outdoor areas for entertaining. From the formal entry hall, one is drawn outside through classic French doors that open onto wide stone steps. Flanked by terra-cotta pots filled with plants in cool shades of blue and white, the steps lead to the inviting reaches of the terrace, and beyond to the garden itself. From the terrace, walled brick steps lead down again to a sweeping lawn planted with specimen trees, including a dramatic, old weeping beech that was successfully

ABOVE. David Easton and Eric Smith use lighting as an element of design. The steps leading into the pool are lit from underneath, creating an inviting sparkle in the night.

FACING PAGE: Shaded by a variety of rare trees and surrounded by thick shrubbery, the bluestone terrace is furnished with black iron furniture crisply upholstered in white.

ABOVE: The artfully aged brick and masonry cooking center and fireplace look as though they came from a French *manoir*. Oriole windows are cut through both chimneys.

moved from the front of the house to make room for a court-yard entry. At the living room end of the terrace, another set of steps leads down to the pool area, with its guest-cum-pool house. The pool area is another important focus for entertaining. Far enough from the other areas, yet a part of the whole, the division of the property into natural spaces for entertaining means that the three daughters of the family can host a pool party while a dinner party is in progress on the terrace. On one side of the pool, oversized, black-painted French iron chaises, each with its own elegant market umbrella, and upholstered in impeccable white, are set with classical precision.

LEFT AND RIGHT: All kinds of seating, from chic wrought iron chaises to old-fashioned wooden benches, fill the terrace, which is used for entertaining all year. Terra cotta containers, filled with a riotous mix of annuals and perennials, with blue and white varieties predominating, surround both the terrace and pool.

RIGHT: Traditional indoor lamps are used to light the "living room" area of the terrace, an area that is adjacent to the actual indoor living room. These lamps are among the many elements Easton and Smith chose in order to deliberately blur the boundaries between interior and outdoor spaces.

THE SCREENING ROOM

ABOVE: Used sparingly, decorative accessories such as this large urn from Treillage in New York draw the eye outward to the gardens, fields, and woodlands beyond the screened-in porch.

FACING PAGE: The porch is filled with antique-white wrought iron chairs, upholstered in a charming topiary print from Quadrille and simple glass-topped tables. These traditional furnishings give this space a timeless feel.

Charlotte Barnes Sickles's outdoor living room is an elegant screened porch that is the perfect appendage to her gracious 1920s stucco home in Greenwich, Connecticut. Original to the house, the porch is also a perfect advertisement for her thriving decorating business. Visitors love the crisp yet comfortable look, one that is simultaneously familiar and innovative.

Her home is an ongoing demonstration of Sickles's firm belief that there are simple solutions to complex design problems. At this home, the screened-in porch is located just off the indoor dining room. It is ideal for the owner's frequent small dinner parties, often just one other couple, or for intimate family breakfasts, a joy every morning from the bright spring days of May right through October. When one finds oneself alone out there, this porch is perfect for reading the paper or simply listening to the abundant birds. At night, she sets big glass hurricane lamps aglow on the antique wrought iron table. The cool simplicity of the space is punctuated by big terra-cotta pots filled with boxwood. Because the porch is small, Sickles sagely keeps decorative accessories and furnishings to a minimum. Summery touches, such as mercury balls set in glass urns and simple bamboo floor matting, keep the focus where it belongs, on the views of the rolling Greenwich countryside, dotted with dogwoods, mature trees, and lush rhododendrons.

Screened-in porches have a timeless feel—and offer a perfect solution to our wanting to experience the outdoors while being protected from insects and the elements. Clearly, they are an idea whose time has come once again.

ABOVE L TO R: Designer Sickles filled her screened-in porch with furnishings usually used indoors, such as club chairs and ottomans upholstered with fabric also from Quadrille. Deft, decorative touches, ivy topiaries in terra cotta pots, urns filled with old mercury balls, intriguing hanging lanterns, and simple glass hurricane lamps all show the presence of a professional designer. Off the sitting room, the flagged terrace, furnished with faux stone chairs from Joe del Greco and plants in large containers, is yet another outdoor venue that is low-maintenence and perfect for entertaining.

A TIMELESS CLASSIC

In all its eighty-eight years, this summer home in Harbor Springs, Michigan, has only had two owners: Mr. Otis, who built and lived in it from 1912 to 1955, and the current owner, who has owned it ever since. When she and her husband bought it, it was decorated to the nines by the local firm of R. & R. Robinson of nearby Petosky, and Naples, Florida. The classic design worked—and has continued to work—for nearly fifty years. Nothing, not even the crisp outdoor upholstery covering the home's original 1912 porch furniture, has been changed.

But this summer home is far from being pickled in aspic. Filled with antique wicker furniture covered in a soothing green that reflects the garden beyond, the porch is the epicenter of summer activity. Because the porch is shady, pots of ivy provide forgiving greenery. From June until after Labor Day, the nonagenerian owner hosts a "real party" once a week, as well as almost daily luncheons and frequent cocktail parties. She has countless visiting family members and friends, and a social calendar that would stymie hostesses half her age.

Beyond the pristine green and white porch, a vast lawn spreads down to Lake Michigan. An old pond is the focal point, an oasis of blue in a sea of green grass. When he was alive, the owner and her husband added old stones and a water jet to the pond.

Each day, this lady of the house walks across her lawn and down to the beach, gathering up sea glass that she places in a glass jar on the center of the wrought iron table on the porch. Down by the water, a frayed flag snaps smartly in the wind. Sometimes she pauses in the rustic overlook that sits atop the steps leading down to the beach, a structure she affectionately calls her "Teahouse of the August Moon," to drink a glass of iced tea as she gazes out over the tranquil lake.

ABOVE: The owner of "Birchwood" in Harbor Springs, Michigan, relaxes in her beloved clapboard, New England-style summer home, which has remained unchanged since the mid-1950s.

FACING PAGE: "Birchwood," as its name implies, is surrounded by stands of birches and lawns that slope gently down to Lake Michigan.

ABOVE L TO R: The porch at "Birchwood" is filled with furniture that looks good as new, despite not having been reupholstered for forty-five years. A small pond, with a splashing fountain, and and underlit reflecting pool, adds to the magical feel of the place. A glass jar filled with wonderful pieces of colored glass graces the porch, each piece found by the owner on her daily walks along the beach.

FACING PAGE: The wooden overlook, built right above the shore, is a perfect place to shelter and look out over the ever-shifting light on the lake.

A perennial garden separates the main lawn from the swimming pool area, a pretty interlude that keeps the pool out of sight. This garden is a favorite noshing spot for local deer, so the delphiniums and monkshood aren't what they used to be. This pool area is another popular summer living space, especially when grandchildren are in residence. There's a small, unimposing pool house that holds an ice box and a bathroom —"It's all you need for entertaining."

When it was first built, the house was surrounded by strong Michigan forest, a northern growth of pine and birch. Mr. Otis took down the pines—but left the arching stand of birches to frame the endless views of Lake Michigan.

WHITE ON WHITE

Set like a jewel in Lake Michigan, Mackinac Island is the quintessential American summer community: Picture pristine white houses clustering along the shore, the sparkling blue of the lake, the spectacular old Grand Hotel, the clop of horses pulling carriages—no cars allowed!

Completed in 1887, the Grand Hotel spurred the development of the surrounding community. Because there was a rail link between Chicago and the ferry to the island, Mackinac rapidly evolved into a beautiful resort area, the most refined in the Midwest. Today, all the houses in the community sit on land that is owned by the state of Michigan, to guarantee that they will be maintained to a high standard.

When this Queen Anne home, begun in 1887 and finished in 1893, was bought in 1988 by a Chicago industrialist and his wife, it was propped up by tree trunks and in serious need of work. To the rescue came Barry BeDour, who is the official restorer of period homes on the island. Working in tandem with the local historian, he transformed the house into a solid, functional home, one that retains its Victorian virtues while working well for the family who live there today.

The commodious porch is furnished with 1920s antique wicker, upholstered in white with deft pastel touches. Pale-blue ceilings reflect the light off the lake. Not only is the porch the virtual living room of this house, each bedroom has a porch as well. A glassed-in area shelters part of the porch, furnished for eating and sitting, from the winds that blow up off the lake. The sun shines in at cocktail hour, adding a grace note to each day.

In the morning, the family greet those passing by, learn the day's local buzz, and arrange the day's social life. The house swarms with visitors, children, and dogs, who love to frolic by the lake and then rest on the porch, watching the world, and especially the horses, go by.

ABOVE: The residents of Mackinac Island, a quintessentially American summer resort, share a collective belief in flying the stars and stripes. All along the lakeshore, flags snap in the wind.

FACING PAGE: This late-nineteenth century American Queen Anne home is one of the community's many architectural gems, with turrets, a great front porch, and upstairs sleeping porches overlooking Lake Michigan.

ABOVE AND BELOW: The glassed-in portion of the porch provides necessary shelter from the harsh winds that often blow across the vast, tidal waters of Lake Michigan, which is just across the street from this house.

ABOVE AND RIGHT: All the outdoor spaces of this home are furnished with antique rattan and wicker, and planters filled with bright red geraniums.

FACING PAGE: Barry BeDour, who has restored many of the architectural grande dames on the island, used a virtual encyclopedia of Victorian details throughout both the exterior and interior of the house.

PRACTICAL MAGIC

ABOVE: Children rule at the Feid home north of New York City. The antique white clapboard poolhouse began life as a playhouse. Planters filled with low-maintenence boxwood and pansies add color all around the property.

Decorator Helen Feid wanted a family home, a home to be lived in. The 1930s white clapboard, originally the caretaker's cottage at "Horseshoe Farm," fit the bill perfectly. About an hour from New York City, it was ideal for this family with three young children. Because it had been added onto several times, the home had the unique architectural possibilities that new homes rarely offer.

The Feids began by turning the attached garage into a family room, a change that helped to create an entry-courtyard garden. Gravel paths surround beds filled with classic plant materials, such as miniature crabapples, myrtle, boxwood, and spruce.

At the back of the house, the kitchen and bedroom wings form a semienclosed patio space. Paved in bluestone, this area has the scale of a large living room. This is where the family live their warm weather lives. It's where bikes are ridden and meals eaten under the striped awnings. The terrace, which faces south, is sunny all day long. The knee-high drystone wall does double duty as a retaining wall, diverting rainwater away from the house and down the hill. The terrace is punctuated by pots and planters brimming with maintenance-free boxwood and pansies, and filled with furniture from Helen's grandmother's house in East Hampton.

The pool and pool house were there when the Feids bought the house. The pool house is a former childrens' playhouse that was moved to its current spot one winter by horse and sleigh. The pool, like the terrace, is an area that manages to combine crisp elegance with no-fuss maintenance. The pool house is perfect for drying wet suits and towels and for housing the beer fridge. An old apple tree, a relic from this home's time as a farm building, shelters a table and chairs, perfect for casual poolside lunches.

LEFT: The Chinese Chippendale furniture is perfect in keeping with the tradtional white clapboard surrounding the courtyard patio.

ABOVE: Decorator Helen Feid was determinded to create an environment that would be both effortless and elegant, a place where all aspects of outdoor life, eating and play, family time and entertaining, are enjoyed to their fullest by children and grown-ups alike. Her practical choices reflect her sense of family and of fun.

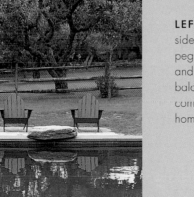

LEFT AND RIGHT: Poolside Adirondack chairs and pegs for drying bathing suits and towels demonstrate the balance of practicality and comfort that is what the Feid home is all about.

THE PERFECT PERGOLA

The traditional, shingled cottage that architect Daniel Romualdez bought in Amagansett presented a raft of daunting problems. The rooms of the cottage were minute, the grounds wildly overgrown. And the side of the house overlooking the adjacent cemetery had no windows.

Romualdez realized that creating a garden terrace would solve several problems at one go. "Since the inside rooms were so small, I decided to extend them into the outdoor space." The renovation included the construction of a single chimney for two new fireplaces, one indoors and one out. The hearth on the terrace provides not only a focal point for the exterior space, but also afforded a solution for several landscaping dilemmas. To let more light into the cottage, the architect added windows along the previously blank wall, which had the added benefit of casting a glow over the terrace at night. He floored the terrace with large bluestone paving bordered with brick. Furnished with oversized wicker armchairs smartly upholstered in blue and white stripes, an ottoman, and a table, the terrace has the feel of a sitting room, open to the stars.

Landscape designer Craig Socia made sure that the terrace functions as garden space as well. The walls are bounded with a trim boxwood hedge. To complement the fabric, he created a border of blue and white flowers, nepeta, heliotrope, monkshood, Japanese anemones, and Pee Gee hydrangeas. As a final touch, Socia flanked the terrace fireplace with two large clay pots filled with pale-blue plumbago.

Extending the length of the house is the pergola dining area, the other key outdoor living area. Its arbor bears a succession of blooming vines, beginning in spring with creamy-pink clematis Montana Rubens, followed by fragrant New Dawn and then Eden climbing roses, all providing beauty and shade down the length of the long dining table. Large pots placed at the base of the pergola echo the blue theme with lacey blossoms of Nikko Blue hydrangeas.

HIS AND HERS

ABOVE: This unusual pool comes right up to the living room, a unique design notion that enhances the owners' sense of privacy while creating a waterfront ambience for the house.

FACING PAGE: The wraparound courtyard, set with metal chaises and large, plant-filled containers, encloses part of the pool area, creating a European sense of seclusion in an area where houses cluster closely together.

When the owners of this house began working with Clemens Bruns Shaub on their home in Windsor, an upscale planned community near Vero Beach, Florida, they had differing opinions about their new home. She desired a sense of enclosure and privacy for her outdoor space yet wanted the feel of her own private ocean in the swimming pool. He craved a sense of openness and a sweeping view of the golf course.

Shaub, who has designed many of the homes at Windsor, easily accommodated them both by lining up the living room, the pool, and the loggia. The pool directly abuts the living room; step out the door and you're in the drink. The loggia is on the far end of the pool. And past that, there is a small garden area with wide, open views of the golf course beyond.

Their mandate for privacy was solved by bilevel louvre doors, which can be closed for seclusion or opened to frame the astonishingly long views that somehow evoke an African landscape. The loggia solves many problems at once, providing additional privacy, a place to catch the breeze, those wonderful, long views—and protection from Florida's sudden storms.

The outdoor fireplace was inspired by those the architect saw in Carmel, California. Outdoor fireplaces are an option taken by many residents of Windsor, who relish both the sociability and the architectural focus they provide.

ABOVE L TO R: At this home, the living room, pool, loggia, and lawn all line up one after the other, carrying the eye outwards, toward the open stretch of the community golf course that lies just beyond the back gate. This archi- tectural slight-of-hand enhances the sense of enclosure and privacy of each home, while simultaneously "borrow- ing" the distant landscape and creating an illusion of limitless space.

THE CLOISTER
AND THE HEARTH

Built on a double property in Windsor, this home boasts a rarity: a completely separate guest house, in a community where most guest quarters are over the garage. Built right up to its property lines, the house, with its careful symmetries and long vistas, is a paradox—that of a home on a grand scale, set on a small piece of property, that has total privacy.

The house is centered around a courtyard space that functions not only as the principal room, but also the quintessential outdoor living room. The high, coffered ceiling and set-in fireplace give the loggia off the entrance a warm, old Mediterranean feel. From the loggia, a lawn extends to the 90-foot-long pool, framed with towering palm trees and luxuriant plumbago set in large urns, framed by intricately paved brick walkways.

At the far end of the property, a cooking/dining pavilion, with its cookstove set into a medieval-looking fireplace and a massive, wooden trestle table, adds a practical footnote to the outdoor way of life that is so treasured at Windsor.

ABOVE: An antique sideboard, tiled foor, and coffered ceiling all reinforce the Mediterranean feeling of this elegant Windsor home, while huge planters filled with sky-blue plumbago add just the right exotic floral touch.

ABOVE L TO R: The high coffered ceiling shelters the cooking/dining area, a space that is in constant use for entertaining when the family is in residence. Brightly colored china, lush greenery, and bamboo placemats all underscore the casual ambience of this outdoor dining room. An exotic, curtained bed from Indonesia makes a perfect play space, a favorite spot for visiting young neighbors.

CLASSIC IDEAS

ABOVE: Fabricated to resemble massive cast stone, this ancient looking chair is actually from Joe del Greco made of featherweight fiberglass. The topiary fabric and potted topiaries further enhance the classic look.

TOP: An eleborate pair of stone urns flanking the steps into the garden embody the classical principle of symmetry.

RIGHT: This floating, instant fountain that moves as it sprays is a lighthearted riff on a tradtional water feature.

LEFT: A wrought-iron tree bench can also encirlce a porch column. **RIGHT:** Designed by David Easton, this simple, black steel balustrade is unusually open to the adjacent view, while still performing its basic function.

ABOVE: Set into a stone wall, this two-tiered fountain gives this space the feel of a medieval cloister.

FACING PAGE: A 1920s European statue evokes the spirit of Rome or Greece. An elegant white fence with its straightforward slats, inverted arch, and ball finials, is a garden classic. The fluted doric columns on this porch are hallmarks of 18th-century neoclassicism.

LEFT: Awnings and curtains transform this patio into a lovely tennis pavilion protected from the sun.

SEATING

There is no longer any such thing as "outdoor" furniture. Exterior pieces are commonly used indoors, and it's not unusual to spot such indoor staples as overstuffed sofas on porches and patios. A new generation of materials, such as weatherproof Sunbrella upholstery fabrics, has created a world of possibilities. Outdoor seatings can be as simple as a hammock strung between trees or deck posts, or as elaborate and "designer" as antique, hooded chaises, or Chinese Chippendale. Gliders and wicker, wrought iron, or French metal are perfect for romantic and classic settings, while twig, Adirondack, and hewn-log pieces are quintessentially rustic. Modern and in-town spaces look terrific furnished in simple teak or metal furniture and glass-topped tables, pared down, with monochromatic or striped upholstery. Found pieces painted with splashes of bright, abstract color, or with flowers or flags are all great ways to announce a whimsical outdoor room.

LEFT: A classic stone bench provides two-way views. **ABOVE:** An inviting striped hammock hung between two trees

1. Rustic wooden bench 2. Metal 1950s spring chair 3. Startling colors in a hooded chair 4. Classic tree-bench provides 360-degree seating. 5. Pink contemporary chair by Philippe Starck 6. Sculptural French metal chaise and chair 7. *Epuipale* chair and primitive bureau give a Southwestern feel. 8. 1950s finds from a flea market 9. Bright-hued riff on Adirondack chairs 10. Bent-willow bonnet chair has a turf seat. 11. Easy-to-move, whimsical wheel-barrow bench 12. Classic Adiron-

dack furniture on a cabin porch **13.** Slipcovered aluminum chairs by Philippe Starck **14.** 1950s French springform chairs **15.** Rough-hewn log and slat furniture **16.** A mix of bright fabrics for a Native American touch **17.** Table made from plywood sheathed in stainless steel **18.** Sunflower chair, a catalogue find **19.** Curved, linear chaise doubles as lawn sculpture.

RUSTIC

The earth is a garden in itself; it doesn't need cultivating. I think that's why I love rustic outdoor spaces so much. Rustic style reminds us—both literally and figuratively—of our roots. Rustic furniture and garden ornaments, with their use of unadorned materials like uncut stone, twigs, and wood, are made to imitate nature. It's a style that answers a very human call—the call of the wild.

A WRITER'S GARDEN

A 1924 Tudor with a rare, walled English garden, a sense of being deep in the country, while only a quick commute to Manhattan—surely it's a dream. That's what two writers thought when they fell in love with their home in lower Westchester.

The first thing the couple did upon taking possession was to add a fourth wall, completely enclosing the garden. Their contractor replicated both the existing walls and the old wooden door that was orginally built into the front one, creating a sequestered place where the owners both write in total quiet and privacy. Walling in the garden had an added bonus—it keeps out the ravenous deer that ravage the surrounding area.

Landscape designer Memory Lewis tackled the space, which was so overgrown with wisteria and roses and junk plants that the basic bones and perimeter of the garden were buried. She began by moving and replanting existing flowers and adding boxwood to define space within the garden, adding smaller boxwoods around the pool. Low-growing yet lush, these do not detract from the view of the ornamental pool itself, accented by an antique fountain that the owners found in Soho. At the owners' request, Lewis added medieval and renaissance plants to reinforce the walled, English feel of the garden.

Inspired by a book on hermit cabins, she enlisted the help of a builder of rustic structures. He constructed two corner pavillions, a bench, and a gazebo, each set a few steps above the grade of the garden to give vertical lift and provide an overview. Built against the house wall, the rustic trellis has pyracanthus growing on it. In the fall, its fiery orange berries light up this perfect secret garden.

ABOVE: A twig bench made by a rustic artisan has been set in a walled corner of this secret garden, a perfect perch for reading, writing, or listening to the birds.

FACING PAGE: Landscape designer Memory Lewis keyed into the Tudor architecture of this Westchester, New York, home by creating a quintessentially English garden, surrounded by tall stone walls, edged in boxwood, and ornamented with an old stone fountain.

ABOVE AND LEFT: An intricately crafted twig gazebo, set at the highest point of the garden, overlooks the pool and fountain. An old wooden door, set into the wall, adds to the "secret garden" feel of this place.

FACING PAGE: Memory Lewis chose varieties of plants that might have been found in a medieval cloister or a renaissance garden to accentuate the old English quality of the outdoor space.

PURE PROVENCAL

ABOVE: A double flight of stone steps, topped by an iron gate, was made from the ruined foundations of an old, burned-out barn. They lead down to the swimming pool.

FACING PAGE: Wesley Stout designed the pool house with its steep roof, dark wooden shutters and doors, and rough-hewn stone exterior to mimic an old French barn. Inside, the space is divided up into changing and practical storage areas.

The crumbling ruins of an old stone barn in suburban Connecticut, once part of a large farm, evoke a different kind of rustic. After a fire destroyed the barn, leaving only the foundation and some walls, the owners decided to build a pool that incorporated the walls. The result, an award-winning project for landscape architect Wesley Stout, is astonishingly European in look and feel, a piece of Provence transplanted to suburban Connecticut.

The owners wanted a functional pool area that would look as natural as possible, one that had a sense of having always been there. Stout sited a tennis court and vegetable garden on the lowest level of the property, the pool on the middle one, and a lawn with an orchard of elegant, ornamental crabapples that are lovely in each season, on the highest level.

The pool can be entered either through an iron gate at one end, or through a twig gate and down an unusual double stone staircase at the other, a structure that has become an intrinsic part of the pool itself. The pool house, built of stone and with dark wooden doors and shutters, looks like a French barn. The front of the pool house, the staircase, and the barn foundations all surround the pool area, creating a private world, a room for summer entertaining for the family's three generations and their guests. A bar, gas grill, and icemaker all add to the ease of making guests feel at home.

Climbing roses, fragrant lavenders, and espaliered apple trees all add to the strong Provencal feel of the pool area. A game of tennis, a dip in the pool, then lunch in this glorious space that recalls summers among the markets and lavender fields of southern France . . . what could be lovelier?

FACING PAGE: Several different seating areas on all three levels of this outdoor space make it a friendly yet flexible place to socialize. Plants that evoke the south of France, such as fragrant lavenders and roses, have been carefully cultivated.

ABOVE AND LEFT: Designed with summer entertaining as a paramount consideration, the multi-levelled outdoor area is shaded by French market umbrellas and has a practical, slate-topped bar and cooking area. Twiggy metal barstools complement the rough-hewn stonework.

ROUGH-HEWN

The town of Montauk at the very tip of Long Island is a windswept and wild place like no other. Walt Whitman loved to walk among the shifting dunes. And Teddy Roosevelt trained the Rough Riders here for combat in the Spanish Civil War.

The Atlantic is vast out here—there's nothing but ocean between Montauk and Portugal. So a compound that is perched on one of its cliffs, overlooking the wide ocean, deserves an impressive entrance.

The owners of this traditional shingle-style compound asked landscape designer Craig Socia to divert the driveway, which originally led to the bedroom cottage, to lead instead to the living and dining areas. In the new space he planted a garden that would thrive in Montauk's heady air and despite its hungry deer population. Socia planted a border of native shadbush, a shrub that loves salt and wind, and clethra (also known as summersweet), an elegant shrub that grows well in challenging environments.

Then he added a sweeping, rustic staircase of rubble stones with grass risers, a flight of steps that leads up to the compound, as well as a pergola in keeping with the rustic theme. With its massive pillars built of rough logs, vine-covered roof timbers, and flagstones set in the lawn, this simple structure affords protection from the intense sun—and forever views out over the rolling Atlantic ocean.

ABOVE: Designer Craig Socia built a broad, sweeping staircase made of rubble stones, salvaged from the Atlantic beach below, a natural appendage to this cottage in windswept Montauk on eastern Long Island.

FACING PAGE: The twisted trunks of native shadbush, planted to complement the wildness of this property line the path leading to the steps.

RIGHT: A sturdy table sits in the pergola, a covered area crafted of rough-hewn logs that are covered with creeping vines and paved with flagstone. This outdoor dining area provides shady respite from the hot Montauk sun and is a perfect spot for gazing out across the roaring ocean.

LEFT: The modest buildings of this shingled compound let the seascape speak for itself.

COMING HOME

It is a human impulse to return to the places where one has been happiest. For this family, that place is Charlevoix, Michigan, a place where they had spent wonderful summers, year after year.

In 1984, they bought a 1940s Earl Young lakehouse. The house is warm and cozy, not far from the village, yet it feels as though it's in the middle of nowhere. The property itself is spectacular, with 240 feet of lakefront viewed through a stand of birches from a twenty-foot perch. Oak and ash, beech and birch, all grow prolifically here. The lure proved irresistible for the owners and eventually they retired to the house year-round.

An unusual aspect of this home is the outdoor entertainment area Young built in 1947. A massive, rough fireplace of stone set in a sunset pattern, with a grill for barbecuing, is set in a stone grotto. The ground is paved with local stone. Young also bound the property with low walls of local stone, laid in a decorative pattern. All summer, these walls come alive with stone planters filled with bright red geraniums.

The call of nature persists down through the generations of this family. The grandchildren carry their tents down the steep slope to the beach, where they sleep away the summer nights.

ABOVE: Michigan artisan Earl Young was famous in and around Charlevoix, Michigan in the 1940s for his homes and outdoor structures built from distinctive local stone.

FACING PAGE: Massive stonework set in a sunset pattern houses the original 1947 barbeque. Dining is alfresco all summer long on the lakeshore.

ABOVE L TO R: Earl Young's unique, asymmetrical, triple chimneys lend this home in the northern woods of Michigan an otherworldly, Hobbit-house appearance. Wooden eaves and beams overhang this home where casement windows have been set deep into the local stone. His consistent use of local stone and wood can be seen throughout the town of Charlevoix.

AS THE TWIG IS BENT...

ABOVE: Anne Roberts created a shelter made from bent willow branches gleaned from the Canadian backwoods where she works and trains budding artisans at Feir Mill Designs.

FACING PAGE: This decorative column, fabricated from western red cedar ornamented with a vertical chevron design, reflects the fact that Roberts' work is more European than Adirondack in its inspiration.

Anne Roberts is a lucky woman—an artist who has found a medium in nature and made it her own. A former fashion designer in Toronto, she moved to the wild woods of Ontario, where she taught herself the fine and ancient art of creating furniture and structures from bent willow.

The Anglo-Saxons' word for willow was "wick," where it was also their word for "life." In prehistoric Europe, willow was used in making primitive fencing, to enclose fields of grain and to pen domestic animals. For Roberts, transforming branches of willow into organic furniture and trellises, tables, fences, and pergolas is a life-enhancing occupation.

At Feir Mill, her workshop, Roberts harks back to her English roots by working in a style that is less twiggy and Adirondack, more elaborate and decorative. Along with willow, she uses cedar and pine, grass, and grapevines. She incorporates such architectural design elements as sunbursts, hearts, and chevrons, and creates unusual structures and furniture, such as willow-appliqued pavilions with copper roofs and intricately woven chairs. Other specialties are her one-of-a-kind garden gates and welcoming woven shelters. Art and nature have formed an alliance with Roberts's practiced hands and unerring eye.

Anne Roberts' sought-after designs range from the simple to the complex, with such unusual architectural applications as Gothic windows or a pair of cedar obelisks topped with charming, carved wooden birds, as well as more common rustic dining sets and intricately woven screens.

FACING PAGE: Roberts' team of gatherers bring back willow and pine, cedar and grapevines from one-hundred-mile radius around the mill. Some forms, such as this extremely simple growing frame, have an ancient, primitive look, as though they have come from a Bronze Age settlement somewhere in northern Europe.

Fresh willow branches are gathered, bundled together and then shaved prior to being soaked and bent into various desired shapes for trellises and pergolas, shelters and furniture. Tree stump-chairs have backs made from bark.

RUSTIC IDEAS

TOP: A simple fence made from cut logs carries the eye into the distance while serving as an effective barrier to deer.

ABOVE: A rustic garden shed, roofed in hand-cut shakes, lends an organic look to this property while holding garden tools and furniture.

ABOVE: A split-rail fence props up climbing roses, a style that works in almost any garden. **CENTER:** A culvert lined with rough stone that winds through this property creates an appealing and effective boundary. **RIGHT:** This simple, arched trellis made from woven twigs is called wattle fencing, a form that evokes ancient Europe.

LEFT: A split-log bench built into a drystack stone wall is a rustic touch that looks as if it grew there. **RIGHT:** An old, weathered table blends perfectly with the stone paving and gray decking.

ABOVE: This fence woven in a herringbone pattern has a fanciful pergola gate, lending both interest and dimensionality.

LEFT: A fanciful wood-and-twig folly, set deep in the woods, is reminscent of Finland or a Russian dacha.

LEFT: The curves of this arched traditional Japanese bridge soften the hashness of the stony landscape.

COOKING

We've been cooking outdoors since the beginning of time, but the process has come a long way since large chunks of wooly mammoth were pitched onto open fires. Primal, caveman urges have given way to sophisticated palates and more advanced cooking needs. Today, our options for al fresco stoves and grills are almost limitless, from inexpensive kettle grills to state-of-the-art Viking cooktops and ovens. Cooking surfaces can be portable or permanently set in impressive masonry fireplaces or purpose-built cooking niches. Because there are many new venting options, cooking areas can be tucked into a patio niche, or proudly prominent, sleek and eye-catching. Whether one is simply grilling fish or vegetables, or baking a foccacia, outdoor food preparation has never been easier—or more well appointed. There are so many choices that no setting, whether whimsical or rustic, classic or romantic, deep in the country or on a high city rooftop, should be without a cooking area that is both easy to use—and good to look at.

1. A brick unit, topped with a slate work area, provides high-tech outdoor cooking space. **2.** Tucked into a brick arch, this area evokes a medieval kitchen. **3.** A fully outfitted poolside kitchen **4.** A rustic stone barbeque **5.** Tropical leaves and exotic fruit set a light mood on a summer table. **6.** An archway shelters a compact kitchen. **7.** A high-tech gas grill provides a moveable feast. **8.** Picnics are one of summer's gifts. **9.** Space under a staircase is used for a vented stove. **10.** An industrial chimney vents an urban woodstove.

I

IN TOWN

Outdoor living spaces are so rare in urban areas; perhaps that rarity is what makes them so desirable. Or perhaps it is the inherent paradox of "country in the city" that makes these spaces so surprising and so lovely. As a landscape designer, I've found urbanites are amazingly inventive when it comes to carving out their outdoor living rooms. And because they tend to be small, every design element in these spaces counts. Each chair and table, every container and plant, are all carefully considered, chosen, and cared for.

FANTASY ISLAND

Mark Mamolen's in-town oasis is almost unimaginable—a house on an island right in Miami Beach. The house was built in 1938, and Mamolen bought it in 1994. He hired Peter Gallo, a self-described "artistic designer builder," to renovate both the house and outdoor areas.

The result is an opulent home surrounded by the sea, with vistas over the water to the city itself, a vision that conjures Oz in its very improbability. When Mamolen first bought the house, he felt that the previous owners had overbuilt the property. His aesthetic goal was to edit and simplify, to emphasize the views over the water and the beauty of the house itself. With Gallo, these goals were accomplished. This home is about living on the water, in an environment that is both tranquil and urban and Mamolen has achieved the best of both worlds.

Gallo transformed the porch/patio area off the living room into a Palladian arched loggia. The house and loggia share a classic, Moorish feel that is ideal for the location. Together, this loggia and the adjacent pool area are the perfect vantage point for enjoying the spectacular sunsets over the Miami skyline. The loggia and the walkways around the pool are paved with local keystone coral. The columns of the loggia are also made from coral that has been artfully aged with a mixture of dirt and Miracle Gro.

Another outdoor living area, the upstairs porch off the guest house, has astonishing views of the pool and bay. A stone bridge arching over the pool lifts the eye while softening the pool's straight lines.

A dock stretching out into the bay evokes the home of Jay Gatsby——and the endless flashing of an elusive green light.

ABOVE: For Mark Mamolen, perched on a keystone wall, the paradoxical notion of living on a tranquil island, just minutes from the bustle of downtown Miami, is a dream come true.

FACING PAGE: From the loggia, the views over the waters of the pool and bay reflect the spectacular sunsets and the twinkling lights of the city of Miami.

CLOCKWISE FROM LEFT
The all day to-ing and fro-ing of boats and the imposing Miami skyline dominate the vistas out over Biscayne Bay, forming the backdrop for almost every vantage point. The loggia, extending out from the living room, has stone paving and scrolled metalwork. Both the loggia and the shade created by the poolside fringe of palms offer welcome respite from the south Florida sun.

FACING PAGE: Builder Peter Gallo artfully aged the coral stone columns of this 1938 palazzo, creating an elegant loggia with Palladian arches. Gallo and Mamolen shared the idea that their essential task was one of emphasizing the vistas by editng out extraneous elements. Architectural embellishments such as a canal with an arched, keystone bridge and pieces of statuary underscore the sense of Mediterranean classicism.

CASTLE IN THE AIR

FACING PAGE: Christopher Radko's astonishing penthouse garden faces south and east looking out over the sylvan stretches of meadows, grasslands, and woodlands of Manhattan's fabled Central Park and the city's skyscrapers beyond. This urban oasis boasts a raised patio and the ultimate ·urban rarity—an actual lawn, which gets replanted each year and is mowed with both a power mower and a Smith & Hawken hand mower.

Christopher Radko's story has joined the annals of America's entreprenurial successes: how he accidentally knocked over his grandmother's Christmas tree breaking her treasured cache of European hand-blown glass ornaments, how he failed to find suitable replacements in this country, how he remorsefully set off for Europe where he found craftsmen still versed in the old techniques of making such ornaments, and how he parlayed these initial replacements into his amazingly successful import business.

The story is the stuff that dreams are made on. In 1997, Christopher Radko realized another dream, creating the urban garden to end all urban gardens. A lover of all things European, especially Versailles and Italy, and anything from the 1930s, such as Art Deco furniture and World's Fair memorabilia, Radko has created a fantasy that looms above the city on Manhattan's Upper West Side, looking out over the green lawns and copses, lakes, ponds, and formal gardens of Central Park.

This garden is modelled after a European-style rooftop garden. Intense color is used extravagantly throughout, with Italianate plantings of pink and fuschia, mauve, purple, scarlet and white, all bursting from containers of varying heights and hues. The rooftop boasts flowering fruit trees, willows, and birches. The garden has a large, old traditional conservatory, a glass-and-metal arched greenhouse where tropical plants winter over, and are then brought outside when the weather gets warm each spring. The greenhouse is filled with potted palms and oleander trees in containers. Many of the containers are made of fiberglass, which do a superb job of masquerading as metal and terra cotta.

Extending over the greenhouse doors, willow trees frame the views of the rooftop and the city beyond. Just outside the greenhouse is a containerized herb garden, which is frequently harvested for cooking. The rooftop is furnished with traditional wicker, upholstered in traditional dark green. Wonder-

ABOVE: An impressive, vine-covered stone water tower with tall, medieval-looking windows sits at one end of this rooftop aerie. Enormous hanging baskets filled with bright annuals and arching willows shelter a teakwood seating arrangement.

ABOVE: An impressive, vine-covered stone water tower with tall, medieval-looking windows sits at one end of this rooftop aerie. Enormous hanging baskets filled with bright annuals and arching willows shelter a teakwood seating arrangement.

FACING PAGE: Simple wicker furniture set in a corner of the well-kept terrace provide a perfect perch for looking out over New York City. Old-fashioned roses climb scrollwork railings, reaching for the sun.

ful old verdigris'd ornaments, salvaged from the Woolworth Building, punctuate the space.

At the far end of Christopher Radko's rooftop garden sits an imposing, medieval-looking stone water tower, with arched windows and carved fretwork, covered in lush creepers. The tower is hung with hanging baskets filled with trailing geraniums and verbena. Topiary spruces, river birches, arborvitae, potted bamboos and ethereal plumbagos, clustered in containers throughout the rooftop, are just a few of the exuberant plantings. Bright roses, pansies, and lush tree peonies herald the arrival of summer in this urban paradise in the sky, while an old, metal armillary dial counts the passing hours.

CLOCKWISE FROM LEFT:
The old-fashioned glass-and-metal conservatory provides the perfect segue between penthouse and garden. Filled appropriately with fragrant oleanders and lush, potted palms, in winter, this greenhouse shelters the garden's exuberant tropicals from the harsh Manhattan winds. The view from one of the arched windows of the water tower, a spectacular sight.

FACING PAGE: Christopher Radko chose traditional green-and-white upholstery to underscore the European feel of his city garden. An astonishing variety of plants, tropicals, annuals , shrubs, trees, and perennials, all thrive in practical, lightweight containers that mimic antique iron, bronze, and terra cotta. Outside a rooftop greenhouse sits a garden of potted herbs, used in myriad ways by Derrell, Radko's butler and *chef de cuisine*.

A ZEN GARDEN

New York City is filled with surprises and serendipitous spaces that never cease to astonish me. This carefully planned and tended twenty- by forty-two-foot Japanese garden is an island of tranquillity on the fifth floor of a townhouse on Manhattan's Upper East Side. Facing south, the garden sits just outside the master bedroom, visible through a double-bay sliding window.

Designed as a "roji," or tea ceremony garden, it was begun in 1987. The Japanese believe that such gardens take seven to ten years to mature, so this one is now approaching its intended state. The garden is based on the very specific principles of dry rock garden design, or "Karasansui," evoking a profound sense of peace and serenity, of nature revered and nature tamed. Perhaps one of the most telling aspects of this garden is the fact that, despite its location in the heart of the city, no other buildings are visible from it.

Incorporating classic Japanese garden elements of stone, water, and plants, each object has been placed with care and deliberation, and with a spiritual and aesthetic function. From the bedroom, an "engawa," or platform, extends out into the garden. To one side, a "Tsukubai," or water basin, filled from a bamboo spout, provides clean water for the ritual purification necessary before beginning the tea ceremony. This low water basin is surrounded by stones on which to crouch while one is washing. Next to the basin is a skylight set into the floor of the garden, which provides light to the rooms below. This glass space, surrounded by iris and black bamboo, is meant to represent a pond.

The middle ground of the space is planted with trees and shrubs, drawing the eye further into the garden, and creating an illusion of great depth. Walking stones, set in diminishing sizes upon marble chips, carry the eye to the end of the path, adding to the garden's sense of depth and perspective, and outlining a clearly defined pathway. Four stone Buddhas have been placed throughout the garden, each one set out of view

ABOVE: A characteristic Zen gardening device involves bending nature to the purpose of creating a harmonious whole. Here, tree branches are trained slowly, weighted down by a river stone.

FACING PAGE: This "Roji" has all the elements of a classic Japanese tea garden—stone, water. and plants—each placed with deliberation.

ABOVE: The water elements in this Manhattan Japanese garden were skillfully fabricated from lightweight lava rock so as not to overly burden the roofbeams of this townhouse.

FACING PAGE: Despite its small size, this garden contains all the requisite elements of the Japanese tea garden, including a hut made from traditional shoji screens. A rich abundance of conifers and bamboos, and impressive sorts of flowering shrubs, rhodendrons, lilacs, and azaleas, as well as a wealth of fragrant climbing roses, fill this garden with tranquil beauty.

of the others. Other traditional Japanese design elements include several different, intricate forms of bamboo fencing.

Such necessary, practical considerations as weight minimization and waterproofing have been dealt with in creative and innovative ways. For instance, the *tsukubai* and water basin were sculpted from lightweight lava rock, while major trees have been spaced so that their weight is skillfully distributed over different support beams.

The variety of plant materials include white pine, dawn redwood, black and golden bamboo, hemlock, and Atlantic cedar. Flowering shrubs, azaleas, rhododendrons, lilacs, and wisteria provide scent and color, while Chapeau, Napoleon, and Buff Beauty climbing roses all thrive in containers on the upstairs roof. In winter, the garden is artfully underlit, with shadows evoking other days and other seasons.

This oasis of Japanese serenity, set amid the bustle of the metropolis, exemplifies the paradox that lies at the heart of each Japanese haiku, or Zen poem, such as this one:

In my ten-foot bamboo hut this spring,
There is nothing: there is everything.
—Sodo

PENTHOUSE CLASSIC

When John and Patti McEnroe called me to consult about designing their terrace, I was initially dismayed. The terrace, a long, narrow space only six feet wide and twenty-five feet long, is situated just off the entrance to their penthouse, a space that was highly visible, but had been neglected. But in the immortal words of the eighteenth-century English landscape architect Capability Brown, there was "great capability for improvement here."

And so I set to work designing the McEnroes' outdoor living room, intent on transforming the space from eyesore to enviable. Despite the terrace's narrow dimensions and awkward length, I realized that I had good bones to work with. The apartment is situated in a grand old building on Central Park West, and it was from this building, with its great reputation and fine old architectural elements, that I took my inspiration. I decided to play up classic attributes in a way that would complement not only the McEnroes' penthouse, but also the building itself. As the space was small, and had the potential to feel constrictive, I chose to incorporate both the walls and the ledge into which the cast iron fence is set vertical design elements.

I began by designing a traditional trellis with a decorative topper panel, to cover the somewhat unattractive yellow-beige brick of the building. At the far end, a short trellis wall now separates the McEnroes' terrace from their neighbors'. To conserve space, I designed a table and bench and a series of planters that would look built-in. The planters are made of teak, which I lined with fiberglass cloth. I filled them halfway with fiberglass peanuts and placed a lightweight soil mixture on top, so as not to add a great deal of weight to the terrace itself, and set a six-foot-long teakwood bench in between. Then I painted everything from the trellises to the furniture and planters the same shade of dark green. Keeping things simple, consistent, and harmonious was key to the design, because the terrace area I was working with was so small.

FACING PAGE: John and Patti McEnroe and their children enjoy the views and air from the newly refurbished terrace of their penthouse on Manhattan's Central Park West.

ABOVE: The long, narrow space presented many design challenges. The primary solution was to bring a sense of openess and verticality, using a combination of climbing plants and tall topiaries.

Next, I set a series of lightweight, fiberglass window boxes that actually look like old, cast bronze along the ledge opposite to the trellis wall. I planted them with small boxwoods, trailing ivy, bright annuals, and morning glories, to climb the old cast iron railings that are built into the ledge. This terrace garden is essentially a green one, with teak planters filled with boxwood, climbing hydrangeas, and ivy. These plants are reliable and low maintenance, excellent choices for a north-facing, urban setting. For splashes of color, I added climbing Eden roses, annuals, and bulbs.

As a finishing touch, I placed a fiberglass urn at the entrance to the terrace, another container that also looks like bronze, planted with a four-tiered boxwood topiary. This planting carries the eye upward, giving needed visual interest and verticality to a space that is essentially linear.

Amazingly, I designed, built, and planted the McEnroe terrace garden in just three weeks. It looks as though it has always been there—and will, I know, get even better over time.

ABOVE: Boxwood planted in lightweight containers that look like authentic Italian terra cotta punctuate the space; while teakwood planters filled with greenery line the painted iron railing.

FACING PAGE: The intricate, custom-designed trelliswork painted in classic dark green, planted with bright annuals, climbing roses, ivy, and morning glories, camouflages an unattractive brick wall.

MANHATTAN TRANSFER

In his penthouse in midtown Manhattan, Andrew Klink, his friend and designer John Carloftis, and landscape designer Miguel Pons have together created a city garden that has evolved into a truly remarkable living space. Spectacular views extend out over the United Nations complex and the Chrysler Building, to neighboring spires and towers, and across the broadness of the East River, with its ever-shifting light. This garden has proven to be a fine replacement for the drought-tolerant Italianate garden in Los Angeles that Klink left eight years ago.

Facing south and east, the 1,500-square-foot space is separated into two distinct areas, a dining/sunbathing area and an entertaining space big enough to hold 150 people. White-brick walls and archways divide the space and frame the stunning views. A retractable awning and market umbrella offer a welcome respite from the bright sun, and an outdoor shower provides still further delights.

Two huge, cast-concrete urns stand at the entrance to the garden, giving the sense that one is entering through a foyer. So skillfully divided is this space that the garden is not visible until one has passed between the urns and entered the gallery area. Other garden containers include black fiberglass containers and standard planters covered in Japanese bamboo fencing for interest and texture.

The wrought iron furniture Andrew brought with him from California is covered in a subtle terra-cotta Sunbrella fabric, which is complemented by classic urns filled with bamboo and a large, iron armillary. Wooden decking and bamboo-covered walls add color, texture, and interest to the space.

The predominantly white garden is planted with wisteria, mulberry, climbing roses, crepe myrtles, and butterfly bush, as well as dwarf white lavender, climbing hydrangeas, espaliered magnolia, lantana, verbena, and Boston ivy.

ABOVE: Such design embellishments as large concrete urns enhance the Italianate ambiance of this garden that contains predominantly white plants, mulberry, wisteria, white lavender, climbing hydrangeas, and roses.

FACING PAGE: Some of the architectural icons of the western world form the backdrop of Andrew Klink's midtown Manhattan roof garden.

ABOVE AND LEFT: Painted white brick arches artfully frame the urban views out over the sparkling East River, while also creating an ideal backdrop for the container and climbing plants.

LEFT AND RIGHT: An espaliered pine and white impatiens contrast richly with the painted brickwork. Andrew Klink, who came to New York after living in Los Angleles, entertains often on the deck.

LEFT AND RIGHT: An antique metal armillary and a pair of huge stone urns are among the many garden ornaments that add architectural interest to this space.

ABOVE: Classic metal furniture adds to the Italianate feeling of this roof garden while a cleverly hung mirror reflects both the surrounding urban towers and the shifting light.

LEFT: A white market umbrella and a pair of crisply uphol-stered chaises offer respite from even the hottest summer day.

IN TOWN IDEAS

TOP: This cleverly designed fence is perfect for a brownstone garden. It maximizes privacy while allowing for an optimum flow of air.

ABOVE: A tiny rooftop greenhouse doubles as a dining room. A baker's rack filled with potted herbs functions as a space-saving vertical garden. **RIGHT:** Urns planted with geraniums add grace to a fire escape.

RIGHT: Planters filled with exuberant strawberries line this narrow terrace, while at the same time holding curving lamps.

RIGHT: Plantings of annuals and ornamental grasses provide privacy for a raised, rooftop lap pool.

ABOVE: English-style planters set on street level change with seasonal plantings.

FAR LEFT: A simple, retractable awning shields a rooftop garden. **LEFT:** A variety of trees frame the views of the urban skyline.

FAR LEFT: Assorted plants in a variety of interesting containers sit on a corner banquette, a space that does triple duty: a shelf for plants, as seating, and as lift-up space for storage.
LEFT: Fountains of grasses and large tropical plants lead the eye out over the Hudson River in this Tribeca penthouse roof garden.

CONTAINERS

Containers filled with bright, healthy plants are the perfect way to bring life and color into our outdoor living rooms. Endless combinations of plants and containers express our tastes and individuality. In a contemporary setting, baskets of woven straw filled with elegant orchids or fiberglass containers that mimic bronze filled with tropical foliage plants, always fill the bill. City folk seem to like bringing the country home, by filling terra-cotta planters to the brim with a mix of annuals and perennials, to move and place as occasion demands. White wooden planters filled with old-fashioned favorites, shrub roses, lobelias, geraniums, and alyssum always add a touch of romance to outdoor areas, while tall urns sporting topiaries and trailing plants, such as vinca, ivy, or helichrysum, lend a classic touch. Pots made of mossy cast stone or twig are just right in rustic settings, while unexpected objects, such as old toy trucks, filled with flowers, are a great way to let your sense of whimsy shine through.

1. Three clay pots of garden grass, a potted lawn 2. A Moroccan painted urn 3. Dense underplantings soften a container 4. Pair of classical cast-iron urns symmetrically frame an entry. 5. An empty container functions as sculpture. 6. A whimsical sculpture of flowerpots and plants. 7. Ivy elephant standing guard. 8. Japanese river rocks fill a container. 9. An old metal gear becomes a small water garden.

1. Cascading plants add interest to a tall topiary. 2. Classic English-style planter with ball finials 3. Concrete planter with weathered paint 4. Wire basket lined with sphagnum moss 5. Clusters of annuals soften an exterior. 6. These antique urns speak for themselves. 7. Low Versailles planters 8. Ceramic urn with bonsai 9. Rustic window box 10. Orchids thrive in an old wooden vessel. 11. Potted palms outside front door 12. Contemporary planters made from stainless steel. 13. Rows of

asparagus fern soften a wall. **14.** A classic cast-iron urn **15.** A mossy stone urn with mythological figures **16.** A Moroccan ceramic urn containing a tree fern **17.** A basket filled with tropical plants **18.** Bamboo trunks of varying heights **19.** A rustic, hollowed out log filled with ferns **20.** Ivy and vinca trail right to the ground. **21.** An old barrow becomes a piece of lawn sculpture.

R
ROMANTIC

"The air," John Cheever once wrote, "smelled as though many beautiful women had walked across the lawn." For me that's the essence of summer. For many of us, furnishing our outdoor spaces gives us an opportunity to express our alter egos and we discover softer, dreamier aspects of ourselves. We begin to crave pale colors and mismatched antiques and develop a fondness for dropping petals and sheer, puddling curtains. Such is the romantic style that captures summer's magic.

RIVERSIDE

For decorator Richard Keith Langham, the opportunity to redo this 1920s Stanford White classic house and pool house in Connecticut was almost more a gift than a job. Purchased in 1995, the property took a full two years to redecorate, but the time was well spent. With its deft professional and tropical touches, the house today is an object lesson in how to live outdoors with grace and humor. As they have four young sons, the family host an informal summer camp, days filled with tennis and swimming, games and contests, five days a week. In winter, when the tennis court freezes over, the boys have skating parties, topped off with hot chocolate around a blazing fire in the outdoor fireplace.

The pool house, hung with coral-striped Sunbrella fabric, is furnished with Chinese Chippendale and rattan pieces from such sources as the Winterthur catalog and Pottery Barn, set cheek-by-jowl with a marble-topped baker's table from London. A spare set of covers, in bright floral 1940s linen, creates a festive setting with bright, new Fiesta Ware dishes.

Just off the kitchen, the breakfast porch, described as a "butler's porch" in the original McKim, Mead, and White plans, is protected by a trellis overgrown with heady honeysuckle and hung with pots of ferns; this is where the family starts their days, weather permitting.

In keeping with her philosophy that life is short and meant to be enjoyed each day to its fullest, the owner uses indoor fabrics outdoors. A porch off the front hall is treated as though it were indoor space, with lamps and a rug, and a ten-foot wicker sofa strewn with pillows.

Down by the river, a tented folly created by Derrell Harris, that changes according to season demarcates yet another outdoor living area. For this family, the boundaries between indoors and out are determined only by nature itself.

ABOVE: Langham updated the magical pool pavillion of this 1920s Stanford White home in Connecticut. Walled in rough local stone, it nestles under a low-slung, sheltering slate roof.

FACING PAGE: Down by the river that runs through the property, a simple awning marks out another outdoor living space, a shelter that changes with each season.

FACING PAGE: Striped upholstery, bright cushions, lush Boston ferns, and potted orchids bring the indoors out.

ABOVE L TO R: Indoor/outdoor distinctions are blurred with the space fully and happily occupied by the four sons of the household and their countless friends. The breakfast porch is an invitingly intimate trellised space. Bright hanging plants and coral-and-white striped awnings provide a vibrant backdrop, while commodious armchairs reinforce the relaxing atmosphere. Cocktails are served, late into the year, down by the riverside.

AN AMERICAN BEAUTY

Like many older Connecticut homes, this 1820s Federal house in Lyme has been added onto over successive generations, giving it not only architectural interest but also a sense of the different families who have lived there. At the present time, decorator Gretchen Mann, her husband, Maury, and their daughter, Molly, are in residence.

A passionate gardener, Mann has planted a perennial garden, which runs along a fence and both screens out the driveway and keeps the pool from view. Filled with lilies, purple monkshood, miniature sunflowers, and lime-green daylilies, the garden's overall cool palette is lit by some vibrant touches.

But it is at the back of this old home that life is lived in earnest by the family and their menagerie of seventy-five animals, including dogs, cats, pigs, horses, llamas, goats, a donkey, an emu, and various fowl, both exotic and domestic. Maury runs his business, Greenwich Publishing, from an out-of-sight building behind the house, a studio built by a former owner.

The screened back porch has a traditional fireplace that is in constant use in spring and fall, warding off chilly evenings. Black bamboo pieces that belonged to Maury's mother are covered in white chenille, an unusual yet remarkably practical upholstery choice. To clean them, Gretchen simply throws them in the washing machine like wet towels.

The porch opens onto a deck, which leads to a bluestone patio surrounding the pool, edged with inexpensive white-painted chaises covered in washable white canvas.

At the far edge of the pool, marked by still more ball topiaries in square planters underplanted with verbenas, geraniums, and potato vines in shades of purple, pink, and white, the outlook is framed by a white wooden gate. Beyond this gate, the view rolls toward distant vistas of the green Connecticut hills.

ABOVE: Bathing suits hung along a fence around the outdoor shower at Gretchen and Maury Mann's antique home in Lyme, Connecticut, reinforce the sense that a real family lives here.

FACING PAGE: Symmetrically placed tiered topiaries are reflected in the tranquility of the pool, while a classic white fence carries the eye over the fields and woodlands beyond the property.

ABOVE: Juniper ball topiaries in stone urns and antique garden sculptures grace the Manns' inviting front porch.

LEFT: Gretchen Mann's fenced perennial garden, lined with gravelled paths, is filled predominantly with white and purple flowers, with touches of yellow and lime.

LEFT: A striking painted wooden tree bench reinforces the elegant, all-American classicism of this early 19th-century Connecticut home.

RIGHT: A plant stand flanked by old columns plays against a white brick wall.

LEFT: White rocking chairs and panelled English planters with elegant ball finials greet visitors. The painted floor lends a traditional touch to the front porch.

RIGHT: Maury, Gretchen, and Molly Mann play with four of their dogs, just a small sampling of their menagerie of some seventy-five animals.

RIGHT: Decorated with whimsical garden artifacts, the antique, stripped wood fireplace on the porch extends the Mann's outdoor living from early spring through late fall.

BELOW: Poolside chaises upholstered in practical—and washable—white chenille are sheltered by market umbrellas. Old stone urns and more of Gretchen Mann's beloved topiaries dot the pool area.

AN ELEMENT
OF SURPRISE

Decorator Jamie Drake of Drake Design shows his romantic colors in his house in the Hamptons. The large, bluestone patio adjacent to the house looks out over a varied landscape from its perch high atop a drystack wall. The setting, with its various levels, lushly planted perennial garden, and long vistas, gives the house and grounds the feel of an English manor.

Because the house sits on the crest of a steeply pitched hill, the wall was added as a necessary antierosion measure, an addition that also gave form and perspective to the property. Prior to the installation of the wall and garden, soil from the hill would run straight into the pool whenever it rained. Designed and installed by Craig Socia, the "ha-ha" wall, a landscaping device first used in the eighteenth century, serves to lessen the sharpness of the drop, while adding still further to the English country house ambience Drake has achieved. On the deck level, which is Drake's outdoor dining room, a hooded chaise and chair evoke hall-porter furniture.

Pots filled with spiral junipers define the edges of the patio, while the base of the house itself is lavishly planted with boxwood, burgundy-leaf potato vine, and a riot of fragrant lilies, cannas, and phlox.

The pool area is furnished with classic Adirondack chairs, each with its own lantern, set under an exotic, fringed purple umbrella from Indonesia. At the very edge of the lawn, bordering the forest that abuts the garden, sits a rustic, two-story folly made of local cedar, a perfect—and romantic—segue from civilization to wilderness.

ABOVE: The fabric-hooded chaise and chair on the deck reinforce the country manor feel of the house.

FACING PAGE: The paved pool area boasts many romantic touches, including elaborate lanterns set next to classic Adirondack chairs, a stone statue, and a fringed umbrella that comes from faraway Indonesia.

SOUTHERN COMFORT

ABOVE: An old garden bench nestles under characteristically romantic southern trees, magnolias and dogwoods, chosen for Garren and Priano by their landscape designer Doug Wood.

FACING PAGE: A birds-eye view of the pool and garden demonstrates the symmetry.

Heading south for the weekend may sound like a bit of a stretch, but for Garren, of the Garren Hair Salon at Henri Bendel in New York City, and his colleague, hair stylist Thom Priano, heading south means heading home. While New York's minions are bucking the traffic to the Hamptons or heading north to Connecticut, Garren and Priano are on a plane, headed for Richmond, Virginia, to their Spanish-style home set in impossibly green lawns.

Visiting friends in 1980, the pair came under the spell of the gentle pace of life in Richmond. Some ten years later, a house the two had seen and admired came on the market, a Mediterranean villa built in the 1930s for a department store magnate in Byrd Park. They couldn't resist.

Committed to the notion that their lives would be lived outdoors to the greatest extent possible, Garren and Thom began by converting a dark back porch into an airy loggia. Filled with an astonishing wealth of orchids, its arched doorways provide an elegant backdrop for the terrace, with its intricate paving and black iron furniture.

Landscape designer Doug Wood was called in to reclaim the garden and pool areas, which had reverted to jungle. Today the pool, which is shaped like an eighteenth-century window, is paved in herringbone-patterned brick and set with iron chaises with striped covers. Planted with formal beds of white impatiens, set with spiraling pots of juniper, and filled with such southern beauties as azaleas and gardenias, the pool area is defined at its far end by a classic pergola covered with richly twisted old wisteria.

Richmond's climate is a gardener's dream. For the green garden, Wood chose traditionally southern plantings, magnolia and dogwood, controlled mounds of boxwood, and espaliered pear trees, plant materials that in their lavish varieties reinforce the Mediterranean feel of the home.

ABOVE L TO R: Arched doorways lead to the paved terrace, with its wrought-iron seating arrangements. Mounds of carefully sculpted boxwood border the lawn, creating an interesting contrast in shades of green, while vines and espalierd pear trees contrast with the white painted wall that borders the property. Everything grows extravagantly in the Virginia countryside, making gardening a joy.

BURGUNDY BLISS

ABOVE: Hamptons landscape designer Craig Socia filled immense containers with richly colored coleus, cannas, bananas, plumbago, and hibiscus, many with a touch of burgundy in their foliage.

FACING PAGE: Architect Eva Growney upholstered the wood chaises lining the pool in a rich shade of burgundy. Their angular forms harmonize with the rectangular, grass-set pavers leading to the pool.

When architect Eva Growney renovated the property of this spec house in the Hamptons, she focused on the pool area, transforming it from humdrum to extraordinary. An alternating pattern of small and larger rectangular bluestones set in the grass leads to the pool itself.

In the new, dormered pool house she designed, Growney created a colorful main room decorated in striking shades of burgundy, fuschia, and orange, with couches for entertaining and a complete kitchen. The brick-paved outdoor dining room, furnished with two square teak tables and chairs from Mecox Gardens, is protected by a deep overhang, supported by solid, craftsmen-style columns. An impressive brick barbecue, with its state-of-the-art Lazy-Man insert, is a key component in this family's poolside entertaining.

Avoiding a predictable color scheme, the designer chose a fabric in deep burgundy for the covers of the poolside chaises, a surprising and effective choice. To go along with this unusual color choice, landscape designer Craig Socia placed massive containers dramatically planted with deep-hued coleus, burgundy-leafed cannas, white hibiscus with pale burgundy stripes, plumbago, and seven-foot banana trees that reach toward the sky.

Near the main house, Socia installed containers of lantanas and, later in the season, hibiscus. He set pots of herbs outside the kitchen and, off the master bedroom, placed pots filled with jessamine trees, plumbago, and silver-leafed helichrysum. Next to the front door, these pots greet visitors with a fragrant mix of plumbago, stephanotis, and jessamine underplanted with coleus.

LEFT AND BELOW: A sleek, bricked cooking area with a slate working area is both practical and attractive. A shady patio, surrounded by sturdy pillars, functions as an outdoor dining room.

LEFT AND FACING PAGE: Craig Socia clustered densely planted containers filled with herbs near the entrance to the kitchen. Potted trees frame the view a colorful, mixed border around the perimeter of the lawn.

The Kampong is a ten-acre botanical garden on Biscayne Bay, in Coconut Grove, Florida, that specializes in rare and unusual plant varieties, fruits, flowering trees, palms, and ornmental plants, a part of the National Tropical Botanical Garden.

It is the former home of Dr. David Fairchild, who was one of America's most distinguished botanists, horticulturalists, and plant collectors. Fairchild and his wife, Marian, a daughter of Alexander Graham Bell, acquired the Florida property in 1916. Fairchild roamed the world, collecting plants on behalf of the U.S. Department of Agriculture. On each trip, he would collect rare and exotic plant species, establishing them on the estate—eventually, the entire world of botany grew around his door.

Kampong, which means "cluster of houses" in Malay, was built for the Fairchilds in 1928 by Clarence Dean. One enters under a carved stone bridge, through which a narrow path, thick with tropical growth, leads directly down to the bay. A traditional, Southeast Asian vermillion gate, into which doors are set, leads to the lovely terrace at the Kampong. On the terrace the interplay of stonework, coffered wood, and red paintwork gives visitors the feeling that they are halfway around the globe. Planters filled with a rich mix of exotic flowering plants, and an elegant Thai Buddha, add to the faraway feel of the place.

Fairchild's gleanings include such botanical wonders as Night-blooming cereus, Malay apple, Tree of Gold, and African tulip, his living, enduring gift to the nation.

ABOVE: A calabash, filled with tropical flowers in intense hues sits near the entrance.

FACING PAGE: A bright, vermillion-painted gateway, transported from Southest Asia by the Fairchilds in the 1920s, welcomes visitors to the house.

ABOVE L TO R: A repository of thousands of plants gathered from around the world, the Kampong is punctuated with Asian architectural elements like this ladder. An ancient stone Buddha underscores the perfect tranquility of the site, as stone-columned, wooden-roofed loggias offer visitors protection from the harsh, south Florida sun. Along with the countless exotic plants David and Marian Fairchild gathered from around the world are such artifacts as this beautiful Southeast Asian gong.

FACING PAGE: A stone path through the Kampong's lush, tropical vegetation opens up to sudden views of sparkling Biscayne Bay.

RAINFOREST RETREAT

Spread out over many acres in south Florida, this rainforest garden is an Eden of rare birds and lush tropical plants, filled with all the heart could long for: pools and ponds, private spaces in which to be alone, and larger ones to share with friends.

The extensive property is surrounded by high stucco walls that have been completely covered with metal grids covered in sphagnum moss, an environment that provides a perfect, ingenious growing environment for a wealth of climbing tropical plants. A large, high waterfall tumbles into the swimming pond, creating a permanent mist over the property that underscores its rainforest feel.

Everywhere one walks, there is something new to discover—an artfully framed vista, an open pergola, a carved swing from Asia set in a rustic wooden frame, an elegant arched terrace, a rough wooden doorway framing yet another view, a hut set on an island in the pond. Teak and rattan furnishings and commodious upstairs verandas add to the Southeast Asian ambience of this home.

The house is literally surrounded by terraces, drawing the life of its inhabitants and its guests deep into the lush outdoors. Upstairs, a series of French doors open onto verandas, offering each indoor bedroom its own outdoor extension. Spaces such as the lavish dining pavilion abound for entertaining, eating, and cooking.

These outdoor living areas offer abundant surprises everywhere one looks. Neatly patterned patios boast intricately laid mosaics; a riot of yellow-flowered climbers greets the eye. The turquoise swimming pool is long and sinuous, reflecting a variety of poolside structures, pavilions, pergolas, and terraces, their images dancing in the blueness.

But perhaps most astounding is the silence of this rainforest space, broken only by the splashing of the falling water and the plaintive cries of tropical birds.

ABOVE: The house of this estate in south Florida has terraces off almost every room, both upstairs and down.

FACING PAGE: Wonderful rare birds flit through the air and call from the trees, while the sound of the waterfall can be heard through the dense canopy of exotic foliage.

ABOVE: In a scene that conjures W. H. Hudson's classic novel, *Green Mansions*, a visitor jumps from the top of the rushing waterfall into the pool below.

BELOW: A series of structures such as this rough archway are dotted throughout the property. These structures serve several functions, providing architectural interest and serving to frame the views.

ABOVE: Exotic South American parrots, toucans, and conyers find peaceful coexistence with native birds, as they fly and call through the canopy of tall palms.

RIGHT: Paved stone pathways and steps twist and wind through the exotic plantings of this walled, South Florida estate, where splashing fountains echo the rush of the waterfall.

ABOVE: Loggias, patios, terraces, and pergolas are set throughout the property, each its own specific rainforest environment, its own combination of views, fragrances, flowers, and sounds

RIGHT: Entertaining is appropriately lavish in this rainforest retreat, with linen-set tables decked with exotic, tropical leaves and flowers. Lavish fruits are always on the menu.

LEFT: The large property is completely surrounded by a high, stucco wall. These have been completely covered with a metal grid upon which lush sphagnum moss grows completely covering its surface.

ROMANTIC IDEAS

ABOVE: This thatched Balinese hut is simplicity itself. With a few pieces of furniture and a few containerized plants, this outdoor dining room looks as though it grew in the landscape.

RIGHT: Claredendron, a lush tropical vine that blooms in two shades of fuschia, grows up a simple, painted ladder.

RIGHT: A gated arbor made from trellising and painted bright white creates the sense of entering a magical space, as if you are about to stumble into a secret garden.

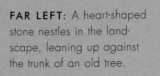

FAR LEFT: A heart-shaped stone nestles in the landscape, leaning up against the trunk of an old tree.

TOP: Unexpected colors, furniture, and fabrics, such as these Chinese Chippendale chairs, with their velvet cushions, and a bright floral chintz tablecloth, can bring a lavish feeling to an outdoor dining room. **RIGHT:** A piece of classic statuary such as this bucolic shepherd boy, will add an elegant touch to any garden.

FAR LEFT: An inviting garden bench becomes a romantic bower when sheltered by its own built-in pergola. **LEFT:** Topiaries, potted plants, and cut flowers, placed in interesting containers such as this ironstone jug, make a lovely table arrangement when clustered together on a table.

LEFT: Fencing created from espaliered fruit trees is a graceful border to any garden.

LIGHTING

Great lighting sets the mood and reinforces the style of each outdoor setting. Today, anything goes: elaborate chandeliers overhang covered terraces, while traditional indoor lighting, such as antique table and standing lamps with wicker or silk shades (perfect for romantic and classic settings), blur the separation between inside and outside living. All kinds of lanterns, simple, traditional Chinese or Japanese ones, Scandinavian modern, Greek fisherman's, elaborate Moroccan ones, can be ideal choices for any setting, either placed on tables or hung from walls or ceilings. Deco torchieres may illuminate modern or in-town spaces. Tall, glass hurricane lamps are great mood-setters, as are whimsical strings of fish- or chili-pepper Christmas lights strung around a porch or threaded through the spokes of a market umbrella. Lighting choices offer a perfect way to stretch the pleasures of being outdoors as the long days of summer fade into evening.

1. Traditional indoor lamps enhance the living-room feel of a terrace. **2.** Bright Japanese paper lanterns cast a romantic glow. **3.** Urban, industrial lighting is right for many modern or in-town settings. **4.** An antique metal candle lamp provides portable light. **5.** Tall lamps on vine-covered posts **6.** Elegant wall-hung lanterns of cut-out metal **7.** A painted wicker lamp next to a wicker basket. **8.** Indonesian lanterns add an exotic feel. **9.** An intricate glass-and-metal chandelier

WHIMSICAL

Whimsy as a quality is ephemeral and difficult to define. But you know it, absolutely, when you see it. Most outdoor environments take themselves so seriously; when I come across one that is totally original, that is full of surprises, and breaks all the rules, I am both amused and delighted. Whether it's an occasional touch such as outrageously painted chairs, a topiary animal, a well-paced whirligig, or an entire humorous and irreverent space, whimsy tells us something important about the person who lives there.

FULL CIRCLE

Designer Jenny Garrigues has extended her 1930s cottage in Palm Beach into a 360-degree series of exterior rooms that completely enclose the house. Connected by a shell path that twists and winds its way through a grove of dense vegetation, these outdoor living rooms take that notion to a whole new level.

Perhaps because she is British and grew up in cold, gray climes, the notion of living outdoors is one that has enormous appeal for Garrigues. Her covered porch, tiled in teal, aqua, and beige set in terra cotta, is furnished with old Florida rattan, painted bright green and upholstered in a body-snatcher, jungle-patterned chintz. A hammock hung from the ceiling evokes faraway places, as do the plantings of palm and bamboo. A zebra-painted table adds yet another touch of whimsy on the porch. A few steps lead down to the pool area, sited parallel to the side of the house. Sunlight dapples the pool area, furnished with umbrellas and crisply striped furniture, peeking through the lush Florida jungle that surrounds the house. On the far side of the pool area is one of Jenny's outdoor bedrooms, a rattan bed that sits right on the grass, perfect for reading and midday dreaming. On a terrace at the back of the cottage, she has created yet another bedroom, this one with an old iron bed, painted dark green and invitingly covered in a vibrant English floral print.

Light filters in softly through the slatted ceiling of the potting shed, with its intricately woven gate. This next outdoor room surrounding Garrigues's cottage has a brick floor and bamboo walls. Water falls from an ornate dolphin into an equally ornate half-shell, providing a cool splashing background of sound in Garrigues's fountain garden. A passionate believer in the ancient Chinese principles of Feng Shui, Jenny is convinced about the healing qualities of falling water.

ABOVE: Designer Jenny Garrigues, a British transplant to Palm Beach, makes outdoor living a high art. Her dream house, "a plantation house in the colonies," is a work in progress.

FACING PAGE: A rattan bed, one of several outdoor bedrooms, sits right on the grass amidst a bower of orchids and tropical foliage, a perfect place to rest, read, or daydream.

ABOVE: An inticately woven, rustic bamboo gate, a lovely touch exemplifying the principles of feng shui, opens into the potting shed.

BELOW: Painted a dark shade of green, an antique iron daybed upholstered in a bright English flowered chintz is yet another perfect place to sit and while away the time.

ABOVE: Orchids sit on a witty, zebra-painted metal table at poolside, proof positive of Jenny's playful spin on decorating and her sure hand and eye.

FACING PAGE: An off-kilter market umbrella, striped chaises, and an unusual old dolphin table decorate the pool area, a sure sign that an antic eye and sensiblity are at work here.

ABOVE L TO R: The veranda of this 1930s Palm Beach cottage is one of Jenny's favorite spaces, an antidote to the cold gray Britain of her youth. She's used a tropical palette of teal, aqua, and beige, and furnished the space with Florida rattan dotted with bright colored cushions. It is, Jenny insists, "a perfect space in which to have dinner as the day fades, perfect for watching the tropical moon rise."

ABOVE L TO R: A mirror, framed in weather-beaten pressed tin, reflects the dense foliage of the tropical paradise and the sunlight dappling through it. It hangs against a simple, white painted board-and-batten exterior wall. The potting shed has a brick floor and is walled in bamboo. It is filled with shifting patterns of filtered light. Jenny uses it not only for its designated function, that of gardening, but also as a peaceful place to sit, a room that combines many indoor and outdoor pleasures.

THE OUTDOOR LIFE

Craig Socia, a landscape designer on eastern Long Island, spends his days intent on improving other people's outdoor environments and on creating perfection wherever he goes. It may be the perfect perennial garden, or the penultimate patio, a pool area to die for, or a lush woodland where only scrub once grew. So when he's home in his own cottage in East Hampton, he revels in having fun on his property, which he has divided up into a series of discrete spaces.

Ask anyone who has one: there is nothing that can compare to an outdoor shower. And for Socia, who labors long and hard, his outdoor *salle de bain* is a necessary joy, and his only shower in this year-round home. Fenced for privacy, and filled with towels and classical statuary, it is a most inviting area.

A blue slate path winding through Socia's property links one outdoor area to the next. The patio right off Socia's kitchen is his main outdoor living space. Furnished with wicker and a dining table, he and his numerous houseguests mingle and eat here whenever possible. Socia not only entertains, he also cooks there, primarily with vegetables from his abundant kitchen garden. The patio is enclosed by a low knee-wall, which separates it from the rest of the outdoors, while not interrupting the view of the greenery beyond.

In addition to his al fresco bath and kitchen/dining room, Socia has also created a designated smoking lounge. Furnished with green Adirondack chairs, and thickly carpeted with grass, this space has an appropriately "clubby" atmosphere.

Socia's sense of whimsy finds expression in his mix of furnishings, such as old wicker and old Adirondack. He often incorporates leftover materials from his landscaping jobs, so that his own property is something of a crazy quilt. A former art director for Ralph Lauren, he has a deep and abiding fondness for flags. Old Glory drapes the coffee table in his outdoor living room, while another is subtly evoked by a wooden set-

ABOVE: Craig Socia, who designs big league, serious outdoor environments on eastern Long Island, is determined to keep his own space lighthearted. Pee Gee hydrangeas bloom with wild abandon.

FACING PAGE: Socia is the Miss Hannigan of the garden world, the keeper and recipient of an immense collection of orphaned and abandoned plant materials. These fill his garden with both color and fragrance.

tee with star-tipped slats. Socia's furnishing and flag touches reinforce the rustic, turn-of-the-century sensibility of his patio.

A great lover of color, he is open and fluid in his approach to his own planting schemes. For him, color is a theme to be played with and experimented with. One year, he may opt for a palette of cool blues and mauves; another, warm yellows and oranges. He uses tons of pots, filled with profuse plantings, especially on his patio. Espaliered jessamine grows as an annual and screens out his grilling area, while two big cement pots filled with ferns anchor the corners of the patio. Baskets filled with bright fuschia, coleus, and setecresay are hung here and there, while an elegant archway of Pee Gee hydrangeas creates a doorway into the landscape.

A pathway of smooth river stones leads to yet another sitting area, furnished with steamer chairs and a hammock, set under an arching old maple. It's hard to imagine a lovelier place to while away a lazy afternoon.

ABOVE: A bent-twig table holds a whimsical collection of bird cottages, irreverantly whimsical English country aviaries made from thatch and twigs.

LEFT: A hammock slung under a shady maple tree is one of Craig's favorite spots to grab forty winks or to just rest from his landscaping labors.

FACING PAGE: A slatted wooden bench with a star-topped back echoes the American flags present in the rest of the garden.

RIGHT: Casablanca lilies and lush hanging baskets are some of the orphaned plants that have found a happy home in this garden.

Pieces of classical garden statuary, piles of thick towels, and an antique cast-metal hatstand and mirror, all fill the outdoor shower, transforming a utilitarian space into a magical one.

In an old apartment building on Greenwich Avenue, right in the heart of the Greenwich, Connecticut, shopping district, decorator Barclay Fryery has created a fully furnished, communal rooftop space that he and his fellow apartment residents share and enjoy.

It all started with Fryery's ingenious notion of borrowing this rooftop space. It would be, he thought, an adventure in living, to colonize this rooftop aerie that had been previously ignored. It could be a great place to enjoy the sun and have lunches and brunches and shared candlelit dinners out under the stars.

His design inspirations for the project were eclectic. The 1960s and the 1970s and the bright cutouts of Henri Matisse led to funky beanbag chairs in bright shades of yellow, red, and purple. Comfortable chaises, shaded by striped canvas awnings, and a wrought iron dining table and chairs add to the indoor/outdoor ambience of the space. Fryery's rooftop gives a decorator's nod to his personal favorites, Elsie de Wolfe, Albert Hadley, and David Hicks.

He designed a series of privacy screens, which he had made of black canvas stretched over frames and attached with ropes, to enable residents to sunbathe and even to enjoy an outdoor shower up on the roof. To tie the huge space together, and give it a sense of visual unity, he commissioned a local pop artist to paint a large oil, a reclining figure outlined in black and colored brightly, an homage to Warhol, Mondrian, and Matisse.

For lighting, Fryery chose lots of glass hurricane lamps along with lanterns from Morocco, which he placed on either side of the treillage. The corners of this large space are defined by containers planted with boxwood.

This communal outdoor living space has just about all the comforts of home: a gas barbecue, piped-in music, and even a

ABOVE: The roof of an old apartment building right in the heart of downtown Greenwich, Connecticut, has been transformed into a communal outdoor space where neighbors mix, mingle, party—and shower.

FACING PAGE: Barclay Fryery, a decorator with a communitarian soul, created a shared space, a project inspired by a group of diverse design gurus.

ABOVE L TO R: Fryery divided the rooftop into private spaces, a shower, some quiet alcoves, and social spaces for communal dining, cooking, and sitting areas. The adjacent skyscape, with its vertical television antennas, water towers, even a resident gargoyle, has become part of the overall decorating scheme. **FACING PAGE:** Tons of potted plants, wrought iron dining furniture, and striped canvas awnings all underscore Fyerey's notion that a shared space should have all the indoor/outdoor comforts of home.

phone. The skyline is punctuated with television antennas and, of course, a brooding gargoyle perched atop a tower.

"Most Americans decorate for show," Fryery observes. "They don't really use all their outdoor spaces." Communal areas are sadly becoming a rarity, a disappearing relic from a friendlier, less fragmented time. Designed for sociability, this rooftop living room demonstrates just how viable shared spaces can be.

MAYBERRY ON ECSTASY

For Miami-based writer Brian Antoni, home is an ongoing series of amusing indoor and outdoor vignettes. He is constantly on the prowl for just the right *objet,* whether it be an abandoned toy or an outrageous piece of furniture, to create his latest fantasy. And from the minute one sets foot on the entrance step, a step set with broken tiles announcing one is about to enter "Chateau Brian," it's a wild ride.

His home, on a corner in the middle of a busy Miami neighborhood, is protected by a dense, tall ficus hedge, a hedge that creates an island of privacy while also serving to soften the fencing. So dense is this hedge that Antoni decided to create a "viewing room," an unhedged area behind the fence from which he greets and mingles with the world as it passes by. The space is demarcated by its own teal-painted door and, in true outdoor living room fashion, is furnished with two chaises and a coffee table. "When I don't feel like interacting with the neighborhood I sit behind the ficus 'curtains.' I can't be on view *all* the time. I need to be able to check in with the world . . . *and* check out!"

Some of Antoni's unusual pieces of furniture include a 1920s wood-and-metal glider, a rusting hulk that came with the house and a piece that had "town dump" written all over it. He refinished it with teal paint. Next to the glider sits a chubby-fish planter, one of Brian's many foraged kiddie toys, which he finds and then takes home and paints. An old, wooden rocker sits on the patio framed by extravagant Florida greenery.

The porch, which Antoni describes as a parody, "a traditional Florida room on acid," has a Sunday painting of Trinidad over the sofa and a green free-form coffee table in the shape of the island, a tribute to his roots on both sides of his family. A sunflower chair, the *ne plus ultra* of High Kitsch, is an object of considerable envy among Antoni's friends. It came from a budget catalog—marked down 80 percent.

ABOVE: A wooden coffee table shaped like an island and painted acid green, along with a painting of Trinidad, evoke Brian's Caribbean roots.

LEFT: An outdoor viewing room, furnished with only two plastic-and-aluminum supermarket chaises, is the chosen venue for holding court and greeting passers-by.

FACING PAGE: Brian ordered this beguiling sunflower chair from a budget catalog. Today this chair has pride of place in this brightly decorated Florida room with its elaborate, wrought iron gates.

RIGHT: A step set with brightly hued, broken ceramic tiles announces the name—and the whimsical humors—of this house, right at the entrance.

MARRAKECH MAGIC

ABOVE: Intense colors, lemon yellows and dazzling Majorelle blue, are dominant design elements in this Moroccan-themed cottage.

FACING PAGE: Painted twin chaises with cushy upholstery and bright, imported pillows are a perfect perch for taking shelter from the sun and listening to the peaceful splash of the fountain.

For a couple of world travelers, discovering a dilapidated old cottage in southern Florida just crying out for attention gave them a perfect opportunity to live out their Moroccan dreams, both indoors and out.

Together with their friend, architect Peter Marino, the Rayners set creating an exotic hideaway. Color is the dominant theme here, mainly the deep cobalt blue seen all over Morocco that has come to be known as bleu Majorelle. This is the primary color of the Villa Oasis outside Marrakech, a home created in the 1930s by artist Jacques Majorelle that today is owned by Yves St. Laurent and Pierre Berge. This blue is so uniquely intense that the Rayners had to import the pigment from Morocco.

The indoor conservatory dining room is linked to the outdoors via a loggia, which reaches into the garden beyond. Although the actual square footage of the outdoor space is small, Marino's flowing design conveys a sense of spaciousness.

Bleu Majorelle is splashed throughout the outdoor living areas of the home, on walls, wicker chaises, armchairs, and shutters. A cool counterpoint is the sea green of the ceramic tiles that have been intricately set in a variety of classic patterns. White walls, upholstery, and columns, touched with pale aqua paint, all tone down the intensity of the primary shades, while touches of lemon yellow evoke the hot desert sun.

As a contrasting touch, the owners chose kneeling-camel lamps, paper parasols, and bright area rugs, all in a clear red. A tiled, eight-point fountain, an important element of the traditional Moroccan garden, splashes softly while a canopy of lush palms whispers overhead. Brass lamps hang from the white fretted woodwork, illuminating the magic of this cottage in the deep Florida night.

LEFT AND RIGHT: An elaborately painted door flanked by imported Moroccan lanterns hints at the cottage's fanciful decor. Sea green handcrafted tiles are both cool to the eye and cool to the touch.

LEFT AND RIGHT: Red paper umbrellas, kneeling camel lamps, and eye-catching scatter rugs all provide a whimsical counterpoint to the elegance of the loggia. A traditional Moroccan fountain, crafted in intricate mosaics in the shape of an eight-pointed star, plays softly in the garden, shaded by rustling palm trees.

ABOVE LEFT AND RIGHT: Umbrellas rest underneath an elaborate window screen. A stone alligator stands guard at one end of the pool.

WHIMSICAL IDEAS

TOP RIGHT: An antique iron daybed, definitely an indoor furnishing, has become an outdoor perch for reading, snoozing, or entertaining.

ABOVE: A stone head gazes over a garden wall.

RIGHT: A rusting tractor becomes part of the land-scape, and as it becomes increasingly overgrown, a kind of topiary.

RIGHT: An arrangement of found objects and flea market finds morphs into an artistic compilation when placed on a clay-tiled table.

LEFT: This painted wood bird is perched in a garden full of outsider art.

RIGHT: A huge, sculpted hand reaches up from surrounding plant materials, as if to catch the sun.

ABOVE: Vines growing in moonshine crocks, set at crazy angles on rough-hewn logs, make for a unique form of garden decorating.

LEFT: At Dianne Benson's house in the Hamptons, oversize hanging pots and overfilled planters embody the principle that there can never be too much of a good thing.

LEFT, MIDDLE, AND TOP LEFT: A Miami collector of outsider art has filled her tropical garden with a strange bird with a rebar neck, a crashed plane, and a motorcycle, all works made by unschooled artists.

ROOF / SHELTER / AWNINGS

The sky above is a lovely notion but protection from the elements is key for outdoor living areas that provide maximum use. Roofing options can be customized to any climate and style, giving just as much—or as little—shelter as each setting calls for. A romantic or classic seaside porch may have a tongue-and-groove wooden ceiling painted to catch the sky or reflect the sea, while a pergola hung with roses or grapevines can provide needed shade. Arches can be rustic or whimsical or geometrically modernist, bare or hung with wisteria or laburnum. Retractable or fixed awnings made from weatherproof fabrics such as Sunbrella, can be plain, floral, or striped, lending a crisp, New England touch or a lush tropical feel. A simple tent or a huge umbrella, a roof or rushes or wooden planks, can be whimsical or rustic, modern or urban. A roofed gazebo or an updated folly offers welcome coolness on the hottest day.

1. A retractable awning offers the option of additional shade. 2. An arched iron walkway feels like a green cathedral. 3. An abstract, open roof frames the sky. 4. Slim logs let in the light in this airy romantic pergola. 5. An entry, created with a series of metal arches, covered in lush bouganvillea vines. 6. A taut, striped awning reinforces the classic feel of a patio. 7. A high, wooden roof supported by sturdy columns covers an elegant patio. 8. Rough-hewn columns are covered with vines in summer. 9. A bare-bones metal frame, lit with fairy lights, shelters the end of a dock. 10. An assymetrical umbrella shades a Florida pool. 11. A roof of logs provides the illusion of shelter. 12. A domed, Moroccan-style gazebo is a cool place to hide from the Florida sun. 13. A sleek, aluminum shade lends a modernist touch.

2 3
6
4 5
7 8

9 10
12 13

11
14 15

THE RESOURCE GUIDE

THE JOHN ROGERS COLLECTION
Available at *exteriordecor.com*

Bring the romance and adventure of the Colonial Far East to your veranda, patio, or poolside. This collection is comprised of classically designed furniture pieces for elegant yet relaxed outdoor living and entertaining. Each piece is made out of solid first-grade European teak. All teak is ethically harvested from the "Well Plantation Teak Forest" and is strictly controlled by the Indonesian government.

PERENNIALS COLLECTION
Available at *exteriordecor.com*

An outstanding collection of fabrics with a sophisticated color palette specifically designed for the outdoor elements. See page 12 for a color photograph.

BURKE COLLECTION
Available at exteriordecor.com

Stansbury Burke, America's foremost distributor of fine fiberglass gardenware, offers classic European reproductions of fountains, urns, and statuary.

Lightweight yet durable, each piece is made of a fiberglass resin compound designed to withstand extreme climate conditions (-10 degrees). Each piece is hand finished by Philippine craftsman in one of six finishes: cast iron, rust, roman stone (faux marble), greystone (weathered concrete), sandstone, and weathered white.

Our thanks to the Sarah P. Duke Gardens of Duke University, Durham, North Carolina, for graciously allowing us to photograph our products in this beautiful setting.

DELGRECO COMPANY

232 East 59th Street
New York, New York 10022
ph: 212-688-5310
fax: 212-688-5207

Joseph Delgreco represents some of the finest designers of outdoor furniture in the world. To the trade only.

FIRST CABIN BENCH:

This classic "landscape" bench from Summit uses first-grade plantation teak and is manufactured using multiple joinery techniques to assure stability for many years of full outdoor exposure.

CLASSIC CHAISE:

Summit reinterprets classical designs, using its modern twist. The Summit Classic Chaise was inspired from the old steamer chairs aboard cruise ships at the early part of the 19th century.

STACKING SUNDECK CHAISE:

The Summit "Sundeck" series is an award-wining design using first grade plantation teak and cast brass hardware.

BRATTLE

Available at exteriordecor.com

The Brattle Company makes fine European-style decorative fencing and yard furnishings in three finishes: white, deep green, and natural cedar. Orders are custom and require at least one month.

UNIQUE STONE

Available at exteriordecor.com

Unique Stone was started by Alex Perakis. He was taught and influenced by his stepfather, Charles Cable. Fascinated with old world statuary, he started reproducing the American and European pieces that he has collected over the years. His technique for aging new pieces is unsurpassed.

CLAYCRAFT

Available at exteriordecor.com

These containers are made of high quality fiberglass; the same is used for automobiles and boats. The finish of most of these pieces has a large amount of metal imbued into their surfaces, giving them the look and feel of true bronze or steel and will develop a patina with age.

MCKINNON & HARRIS, INC. (RIGHT)

P.O. Box 4885
Richmond, Virginia 23220
ph: 804-358-2385

McKinnon & Harris, Inc., has been manufacturing garden seats and tables since 1989. Their "Living Room Furniture for the Garden" is guaranteed for life and is noted for its finish, joinery, and aircraft-grade aluminum alloys.

ROMANOFF PRODUCTS

Available at exteriordecor.com

Manufacturer and distributor of products for the home, office, school, and industrial markets, Romanoff has introduced these all-weather plastic stacking chairs in a rainbow of colors.

CHICAGO TEXTILE

Available at exteriordecor.com

Chicago Textile brings a modern slant to seating. Their trademark "Puff Chair" is inflatable, comfortable, colorful, and easily stored when not in use.

EARTHLY THINGS

Available at exteriordecor.com

Earthly Things is the creator of a prize-winning stainless steel potting table designed to be multifunctional for the gardener and the entertainer. It is available in unpainted or painted steel with stainless steel surfaces for potting and flower arranging. With a quick swap of the tools, you can use the table for entertaining. Under the top shelf is a faucet that hooks easily to a garden hose or any water source. Accessories include two styles of slide-on side baskets and a wineglass rack.

PANGAEA TRADING

Available at exteriordecor.com

Pangaea Trading specializes in affordable, yet practical furniture items. Metal chairs and tables that either fold or stack and have a certain simplicity of design are their signature.

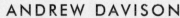

ANDREW DAVISON

Available at exteriordecor.com

Andrew Davison screens striped patterns taken directly from his pottery designs onto 50/50 cotton-poly ducking to make these outdoor pillows. Sizes are 16″, 18″, 22″, and 24″ square and come in red/crème, blue/crème, sage/crème, and mahogany/palm.

THREE COINS

Three Coins Imports is a business owned by Gordon and Linda Ramsey that imports fine aluminum reproductions of antique cast-iron furniture, fountains, and lamps.

SYCAMORE CREEK

The Sycamore Creek workshop is located in New York's rural Hudson Valley. In their barn, amid rolling hillsides and tree-lined streams, they handcraft a unique line of original design copper furnishings for garden and home, specializing in trellises and arbors. Made of copper piping, the pieces are sturdy but maintain a lightweight elegance.

MEYER IMPORTS

215 Frobisher Drive
Waterloo, ON, Canada N2V 2G4
ph: 519-888-6150
800-267-8562
fax: 519-888-7191

Importers of European garden products to North America, from basic pot covers, clocks, and urns to architectural obelisks, trellises, flower buckets, and watering cans.

PHILLIPS COLLECTION

Available at exteriordecor.com

Mark Phillips began this unique selection of garden imports ten years ago and built it into one of the largest selections of such objects available.

DURASOL SYSTEMS, INC.

197 Stone Castle Road
Rock Tavern, NY 12575
ph: 914-778-1000
888-822-0383
www.durasol.com

America's #1 selling brand of retractable awnings. Durasol awnings are custom-made with over 200 colors and patterns to choose from. Visit durasol.com for the dealer nearest you.

ANAMESE GARDEN POTS

Available at exteriordecor.com
18080 La Motte Road
Welsh, Louisiana 70591
ph: 337-734-3656
fax: 318-734-3666

Anamese garden pots are handmade glazed garden pottery from Vietnam.

ANTHROPOLOGIE

1700 Sansom Street
Philadelphia, PA 19103
ph: 800-309-2500
www.anthropologie.com

Anthropologie offers an original mix of women's apparel, decorative garden accessories, cosmetics, furniture, home furnishings, and gifts. To find the nearest store or to request a catalog contact 800-309-2500.

TRICONFORT

200 Lexington Avenue, #701
New York, NY 10016
ph: 212-685-7035
fax: 212-447-1835

Triconfort furniture in laquered resin is designed to withstand the most severe climates and the sun's UV rays. The Riviera and Elysee ranges will enhance your outdoor areas any time of the year.

CAMPANIA

401 Fairview Avenue
Quakertown, PA 18951
ph: 215-538-1106
fax: 215-538-2522

Campania is a family-owned business in Pennsylvania that specializes in reproductions and designs of their own creation that have a vintage "Italian" feel and are made of molded stone.

CULTURAL INTRIGUE

45 Flat Street
Brattleboro, Vermont 05301
ph: 802-254-7422

Designers and importers of Asian paper products.

BROWN JORDAN
9860 Gidley Street
El Monte, CA 91731
ph: 626-443-8971
fax: 626-575-0126

In 1948, Mr. Brown introduced a new design named "leisure" made of welded and tubular aluminum and vinyl lace seating for full-time outdoor use. This design began a new category of outdoor furniture and ultimately, a new industry.

TREILLAGE
(RIGHT AND BELOW)
418 East 75th Street
New York, NY 10021
ph: 212-535-2288
fax: 212-517-6589

Treillage focuses on antiques and decorations for the garden, including furniture, statuary, urns, pots, and fountains. They also move "indoors" and offer the same feeling for home or conservatory with the garden look.